Chapter 1: Understanding th(

Symbols surround us, and we use them to convey meaning
of our existence and are used to help us navigate through the many choices
we face daily. Symbols have meanings, and sometimes they are obvious.
Road signs are used to convey simple instructions or dangers relevant to the
area they are placed. Shop signs use symbols to attract customers, and certain
manufacturers use logos and symbols to represent their brand and make it
immediately recognizable.

Perhaps the most influential symbol of all is the cross. It is an archetype
found in most cultures that far exceed the Christian faith. In Christianity, it
represents the cross on which Jesus was crucified and his rebirth as the Son
of God. In more pagan beliefs, it represents the four elements and their power
in magic and nature. The cross represents the meeting of the spiritual and
natural worlds and is often depicted with a fire in the center.

In Aztec religions, the feathered serpent symbolized the creator god in the
sign of a cross, while the weather goddess also carried a cross. Norse holy
men carried staffs fashioned in the shape of a cross, and Native Americans

marked their sacred boundaries with a cross symbol.

Visual symbols are powerful sources of meaning and can convey a message that unites us all in their feelings. The red and white stripes on the American flag represent strength and courage to patriots and evoke powerful feelings of allegiance, much like flags from other nations do for their populations. Symbols are often used to sum up an expression and replace the written word. The use of emojis, gifs, and other symbols in modern communication is a fun way to tell somebody how you're feeling or what you're doing, which appeals to the fast pace we live.

Popular Symbols That Have Become Iconic

Logos are designed to communicate a message to the customer. They evoke a plethora of emotions and create a visual image to make the customer feel safe and protected when they choose the company represented by the logo. We are preprogrammed to respond to certain elements like color and geometric shapes as humans. Red is a passionate color, while blue expresses a sense of calm and maturity. The best and most iconic logos are simple yet unconventional. Their designers have thought outside the box and created a design that encapsulates what the company stands for and makes them instantly recognizable.

- **The Apple Logo**

  This classic apple shape with a bite has been associated with the wordplay between bytes and a bite. However, Steve Jobs dispelled this theory in 1991. He told a press conference that he simply loved apples and eating them, but the main reason was that they represented the brand's simplicity. The link between this highly sophisticated brand and the simple apple, first seen in the Garden of Eden, has proved that simple images work the best.

- **Shell**

And the logo is . . . a shell. Formerly a black and white image, the addition of red and yellow makes this logo pop.

- **Firefox**

A planet surrounded by a golden swirl of light that looks like a blazing fire of heat and power. Have you ever looked at it and seen the fox? The golden flames are subtly designed to look like a fox's back, and the flames are its tail. The color blue instantly makes you think of Earth and the golden yellow of excitement and passion.

- **The Nike Swoosh**

This logo is an example of one of the most iconic uses of symbolism. It is simple and effective. The symbol derives from Greek mythology and represents the Goddess of Victory – which is apt, as the logo represents sportswear.

While many logos and symbols also include the company's name, these logos show the power of symbols and how they speak to our subconscious.

Symbols in the Occult

Although occult practices aren't a common event, the symbols used in occultism are still used worldwide. Does this mean we are all secretly connected to the dark side without our knowledge? No, it just means that some symbols have transcended their original meanings and have become the art of the mainstream symbolism we see every day.

- **The Pentagram**

  This is perhaps the most recognizable symbol used by pagans and Wiccans. It represents the magical elements of the world combined with the sense of self or spirit. Used to protect and ward away evil, it is a powerful sign of protection for some, but others see it as a simple geometric shape. The five-point star is usually enclosed in a circle and is generally used to represent magical areas that are safe to use.

- **The Hexagram**

Known as the Star of David in Judaism, the symbol is a star made of two intersecting equilateral triangles. The symbol represents polarity and signals the union of male and female energies. The triangle with the ascending apex is the male part, while the triangle with the downward apex is female. It can also signal the joining of spiritual and physical realms. The downward apex represents the heavens reaching down and connecting with the physical world.

- **The Eye of Providence**

Also known as the all-seeing eye, this powerful symbol is a human eye in a triangle or an ellipse, depending on the cultural reference. Visitors to Tukey will often return home with souvenirs depicting the eye to decorate and protect their home. It has been in existence since ancient times and is meant to symbolize divine reverence. It has long been associated with benevolence from more powerful sources and rarely depicts dark or satanic beings.

In modern times it is more closely associated with the rise of the US as a superpower and is depicted on the back of the dollar bill. Some associate it as the ultimate symbol of the way the world has progressed and the surveillance we are all subjected to. It is used as a symbol of the Defense Advanced Research Project Agency, responsible for the rise in mass surveillance in the US. In this way, the all-seeing eye now seems to represent a force that is more concerned with punishing those who do wrong rather than protecting them.

- **Yin and Yang**

Another two-part symbol represents two major forces coming together in harmony to create strength. Two halves create a whole, the concept originally used in Taoism consisting of a circle divided into half by a curved line. The black half is the yin, and the white half is the yang. The dark half is the female representation of the harder negative aspects of the world, while the white is the male counterpart that stands for positivity, warmth, and peace. Each color has a dot in the opposing half, which means they share an inherent wholeness. Because of this, the symbol is acclaimed as the core of unity and togetherness.

- **The Celtic Cross**

Often mistaken as a manifestation of the Christian cross, this symbol is also known as the Irish cross because its roots are in Ireland and can be traced back to the 9th Century. The traditional cross is adorned with a ring divided into four semi-circles. Some experts believe that early versions of the cross originated because the first wooden structures required support which led to the small wooden pieces that formed the struts to keep the cross in place.

Examples of the Celtic cross are found worldwide and appear as simple representations of the form. There are some adorned examples which include illustrations of the Celtic knot and the Tree of Life to make them more appealing and decorative.

- **Nero's Cross**

This symbol has been adapted to represent the Peace Movement, but its origins are biblical. It is an inverted broken cross that incorporates a circle to represent the vision of Nero, which was to destroy Christianity to bring peace. Some experts believe it symbolizes the upside-down cross on which Nero crucified St. Peter, making it a significant symbol of humility in faith. Also known as the sign of the "broken jew," it represents despair at the fate of humankind or the death of a man.

- **The Leviathan Cross**

Also referred to as "Satan's Cross," it is a double cross resting on an infinity symbol. It symbolizes sulfur, an element often connected with Satan or the Devil. However, it had no historical association with the Devil until the 1960s, when it was widely used by Anton LaVey, who wrote his own version of a Satanic Bible. Before this association, the

Leviathan Cross represented the Knights Templar.

- **Chaos Magick**

While the symbolism is associated with occult magic and other forms of folk magic, it has transcended the age to emerge as a new concept that began with the English artist and occultist Austin Osman Spare. He focused his artistic talents on symbolism and was responsible for some spectacular works featuring torturous images and representations of the occult. He was set to achieve fame and fortune with his macabre paintings and works of art; however, fashion changed, and England became disinterested in all things Victorian and the occult. He was sent back to a life of poverty just when it seemed he would become the next wunderkind of the art world.

His work started to regain interest in the 1970s, over a decade after his death. The images and concepts he created illustrated a new form of work called chaos magick. It combined all the grassroots intentions of magic practices to form a belief-based process where your faith in your beliefs is as important as any tool you have in your witchcraft armory.

Chaos magick encourages its followers to draw strength from all forms of magic and use the powers and tools from various cultures to create a Frankenstein monster-like vision of their desires and needs. Creating personal sigils is a part of the process, and using them to work with energy helps you focus on your goals. It uses the process of gnosis to imbue items with the power of magick. In theory, this means that even a simple pencil or piece of string could be made sacred by you pushing your belief into the item and making it magical.

Is it dangerous? All forms of magic have risks, but their impact on you depends entirely on your work. If you're careless, then your deconstructed reality may cause you harm. Because chaos magick is a philosophical approach, it differs from practitioner to practitioner, but in a nutshell, it is the concept that all reality is a liquid state. Chaos magicians wear their beliefs as a mask to navigate and change reality to suit their needs. Define your intentions, and then create the energy to make them happen.

Collective communities have created belief structures through time. Strength and power from believing in a common goal or structure have created miasmas of energy that result in spectacular results and "magic" in a supportive environment. Solo practitioners need to remove limiting beliefs and have different methods to achieve their goals. They can release the power of their inner child and use spiritual guides and support to strengthen their will. Chaos magick is the ultimate law of attraction and focuses on the users' goals and dreams.

Other Meaningful Symbols

- **The Triple Moon Symbol**

A full moon in the center with a waxing crescent moon on the right and a waning crescent moon on the left, this symbol is the epitome of feminine energy. Use it to attract the divine energy of womanhood and celebrate the Goddess in her three aspects, the maiden, the mother, and the crone.

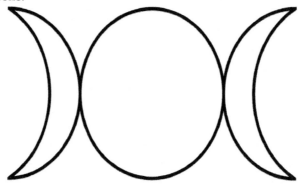

Covens and witches use this symbol to draw strength and empowerment to spells and rituals. Use it to boost confidence when you feel down and stuck in a rut. Use the wisdom it symbolizes to attract powerful energy into your life.

- **The Aether Symbol**

Also known as the spirit or the ether, the symbol resembles a cartwheel and represents space and balance. Ancient Greeks believed it was a plane of earth that was higher than our physical world, and it governed the laws of gravity. The spirit element is often referred to as the glue of the gods, and the symbol used to create a pathway between the heavenly realms and earth. In our physical bodies, it represents the union of heart and soul.

Use this symbol when practicing divination to strengthen your connections and channel the spirits. It will encourage new messages and a stronger bond to the spirit world.

- **The Horned God Symbol**

The horned god symbol is a full moon topped by a crescent moon, representing the essence of male energy. The image is filled with the power of the hunt and is used in rituals for fertility and virility. In Wiccan terms, the horned god impregnates the goddess in winter and gives her the fecundity to thrive through the year and bring forth her bountiful gifts. Use this symbol to attract wealth, masculine energy, and strength.

- **The Labyrinth**

The image of a circular maze represents the path to divinity and is perceived as a sign of wholeness. The winding pattern signifies the journey made to achieve spirituality and interconnection with the cosmic order and the higher beings that guide us. Use the labyrinth to help you meditate and discover the encoded knowledge within your DNA. The symbol is also used as a trap to capture negative energy and bad spirits within.

- **The Hand of Fatima**

A powerful pagan symbol, the hand of Fatima is a five-pointed open hand with an all-seeing eye in the palm. It is dedicated to the daughter of the Prophet Mohammed and is used to ward off evil and keep your home safe. It attracts wealth and abundance and represents the true energy of peace and goodness.

- **The Sigil of Lucifer**

Originating in the Grimoire of Truth, the symbol is attributed to the dark lord's power on earth. Composed of an inverted triangle and a V at the bottom, the overall impression is of a chalice representing the Creation's strength. While some practitioners use it to connect with the fallen angel, others believe it has powerful significance in today's society.

The symbol represents freedom and independence. As an angel, Lucifer was the only angel to stand up to the Almighty and take the consequences of deciding his destiny. It also represents wisdom and celebrates the intelligence and wisdom of the brightest angel in the Kingdom. This sigil is a good example of how the meanings have been misinterpreted because of historical associations. The meanings are positive, but most people avoid them because of the satanic ties.

- **The Horned Hand**

Commonly associated with rock bands today, the horned hand is a gesture that has the thumb flat against the palm and the middle and ring finger bent over to touch it. The remaining fingers are held aloft and defiant. Today it means "rock on" or other music-based greetings, but the history behind the gesture is more complex.

In historical terms, the raised index and pinky fingers represented the horns of the wooly goat of Mendes and were used to show allegiance to the occult. In modern terms, it is used to ward off evil and banish unwanted energy and is also a symbol of membership.

- **The Ouroboros**

The formation of a circle with a snake or dragon biting its tail is a highly recognizable symbol originating in Ancient Egypt. It represents the cycle of life and has universal interpretations regardless of religious associations. Use it to symbolize new life or the end of a cycle. The snake's skin is shed to give birth to new beginnings, just like we shed layers of ourselves to evolve.

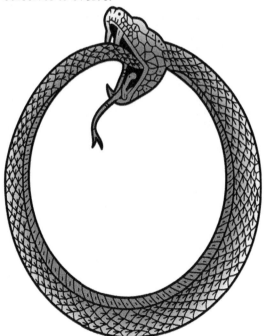

Occult symbols are subject to different interpretations, and we should always consider other people's feelings when using them.

Chapter 2: The Angelic Sigils

Archangel sigils are the mark of the angels that rule the seven Heavens. They are representative of a signature and are formed by spelling out the angel's name on a Rose Wheel or Cross that contains letters and combinations of letters in sections. Templates for the Rose Cross can be found online in Hebrew and English versions. Creating a shape based on the angels' names forms a sigil that can be used as a magickal key to invoke the power of the angel you call upon.

The sigils created by both English and Hebrew interpretations are successful and will connect you to your chosen angel. Create a sigil that corresponds to your guardian angel or connect with the powerful archangels using their sigils.

Archangels and How They Can Help You

Archangels are depicted as female and male energies and aren't restricted or defined by gender. When you interact with them, they can adapt their energy depending on the nature of your message.

- **Archangel Gabriel**

The strong and divine messenger who is the conduit of God, he imparts strength and solid energy and is one of the most popular and approachable angels in God's realm. His name stands for the "strength of God," and he appears in both the Old and New Testaments.

- **Archangel eel**

Michael is the protector of Heaven and is renowned for his courage and strength. He is the celestial slayer of dragoons and is often pictured with a sword and shield. He can be called upon to shield you from physical and astral attacks and fight for you when you feel abandoned. Michael will be the rock you can rely on and who will stand by you whenever you need him. Archangel Michael believes in the power of good and will reward anybody who lives a pure life with his protection. When the Day of Judgement dawns, Michael's task will be to weigh human souls on the divine scales.

- **Archangel Metatron**

The keeper of the Book of Life, Metatron, is the official bookkeeper of the Heavens. He keeps records of your good deeds and is responsible for maintaining a log of what is happening in Heaven. Interact with Metatron to raise your vibration and achieve a state of joy and love. He will help you block negative sources and understand the impact of positivity. The things you ingest and use can change your vibrational state, so replacing negative items and activities with healthier information will make you feel more attuned to the positive energy around you. This lifts your spirits and makes you more receptive to connections that will benefit your life.

- **Archangel Raphael**

His name means "healing," and Raphael is responsible for healing the ills of man. He works with the medical community and is the patron angel of medical experts, including nurses and doctors. Call on him when you need healing; physical, mental, and spiritual wounds are all part of his remit, and he will give you the compassion and guidance to find relief. Raphael can also be called upon to help you heal from grief at the suffering of others, and he helps caregivers and relatives of the sick.

- **Archangel Ariel**

The Lioness of God Ariel is the angel tasked with overseeing the natural world. She cares deeply for animals and all things associated with nature. Her powers help people involved with conservation and ecological projects, so invoke her power if you feel the same affinity with the planet and those who live here. Her powerful force is dedicated to helping you achieve your dreams and attain the physical and mental abundance you crave.

- **Archangel Haniel**

One of the most approachable archangels, Haniel, is known as the Grace of God. Her energy helps women heal when they have problems with fertility and menstruation. She encourages humans to connect with the heavenly energy and benefit from celestial forces as they seek their higher purposes. Haniel encourages people to develop their natural talent for clairvoyance and will protect their souls throughout their lifetime and beyond.

- **Archangel Jophiel**

The angel of wisdom and beauty is often portrayed as a glorious raven-haired female with a strong and kind face. She is the angel who works with creatives and encourages them to produce works of art and music that bring joy to the world. If you're in turmoil and can't find a way out of chaos, appeal to Jophiel to calm emotional stress and restore harmony. Jophiel will guide you to safety when all your roads seem to lead to danger.

- **Archangel Muriel**

The "perfume of God" Muriel is often depicted as a fair-haired young woman with a stunning countenance and a pure appearance. Call on her when you feel emotionally adrift, and her compassion and love will make you feel like you're never alone. Muriel is the emotional support we all need, and her calm energy is available to all who call on her.

- **Archangel Uriel**

In the illuminating light of the heavens, Uriel stands close to God and is one of his illuminated seraphim. He can help you when you're struggling with darkness and confusion, and his energy will direct you to a solution and insight into what you need to do next. He is a source of higher energy and can help you connect with your higher self to achieve enlightenment.

- **Archangel Azrael**

The angel of death may seem like a dark and foreboding figure, and his depiction is often surrounded by darkness and shadows, but he is the angel responsible for spiritual counseling. If you lose a loved one or are facing death yourself, he will help you deal with the stress and mental strain of grief. His energy is available when you need it the most, and he is always on hand to guide you through the dark. Azrael is there for you when you have dangerous thoughts and feel like you're on a path to destruction; he understands that mental anguish can lead to harmful intent, and he will guide you towards the light.

- **Archangel Zadkiel**

The angel of forgiveness and mercy, you should turn to Zadkiel when you need to forgive others who have done you harm. He will help you rid yourself of negativity and leave your past behind. His high vibrational energy will lift you and fill you with the cleansing light of the Heavens. You will move on, and the past will stay where it is and cease to impact you negatively. Ask him for assistance in cleansing your spirit and gaining the freedom to progress.

- **Archangel Chamuel**

The angel of peace will help you resolve conflicts and become more relatable. She will give you the tools to become a better communicator and achieve improved relationships both on earth and in the spiritual realm. She gives you the confidence to become a better friend and partner who understands how satisfying it is to help others. If you feel sad and stuck in a rut, ask her to help you move on and rejoin society. You will know when she is near you because you will feel a tingling sensation in your limbs, like pleasant pins and needles.

- **Archangel Jeremiel**

The quiet angel Jeremiel finds communicating with humans more complex than other angels. His style is more laid back and less vocal, preferring to convey his messages using mental images, dreams, and visual signs instead of verbal communications. He is just as dedicated as the other angels but is more likely to be waiting in the wings for those individuals who will benefit the most from his quieter energy. He works with the unconscious mind and will visit you when you need him the most to restore your connection with the light of Heaven.

- **Archangel Raziel**

He is God's secret keeper and one of the most enigmatic angels in the Heavenly realm. His peaceful and calm nature means he is very hard to detect even when standing by your side. Raziel is a powerful angel who guides those who want to improve their psychic and spiritual aspects. Knowing yourself is the key part of self-improvement, and Raziel will work with you to discover your strengths and improve your communication skills.

- **Archangel Sandalphon**

This archangel is the cosmic "man of the people" and is one of the easiest angels to work with. His matter-of-fact energy means he is available to be your personal link to the heavens. When you work with Sandalphon, you will feel like you have made a new BFF who happens to have the power to make sure the universe answers your prayers. Sandalphon is a gentle soul who loves animals and nature and can help you form natural connections with the earth.

- **Archangel Sachiel**

The archangel of wealth and success works well with businessmen, entrepreneurs, lawyers, and judges. His interests in legal affairs and justice mean he will help you with legal and business issues. His name means the "covering of God, "and you can pray to him to bring you power and abundance. He will show you how to attract new and successful friendships and increase your social prestige. He is associated with the planet Jupiter, the largest planet in the solar system, and will inspire you to evolve and grow to achieve success.

- **Archangel Orion**

He is named after the brightest star in the sky and shines from within. He isn't depicted as an angel of light; he is often in the shadows, but his pure energy is the reason behind his name. Your dreams and hopes are known to him, and he will work with you to get what you want and realize your dreams. Orion works with humans by sending his unique vibration and filling you with love and kindness.

How to Learn Which Archangel Is Best for You

Studying the strengths of the angels should help you choose whom to reach out to. Saying prayers to your chosen angel will help you connect, and personalizing your messages with the sigil associated with them will strengthen your call for help. If you're unsure who your angel should be, look for signs around you. The name Michael or Raphael may start to appear in your environment, or you may hear music that reminds you of your angel.

Pay Attention to Your Intuition

Have you ever had a hunch or an idea that just happened to work out? That's a sign your intuition is surfacing. Your intuition is your inner voice, and it comes from your soul; just like a muscle, it needs to be exercised and flexed regularly. If you ignore your intuition, it will cease to work for you, and you will lose a powerful part of your inner sense. Most people use their intuition without realizing it and are guided to the best paths for them.

Divine intuition is when your vibration connects with an angel's intuition, and you receive divine guidance to help you overcome your obstacles and issues. All you must do is ask them to work with you, and it will happen. When you open your heart to the angels, they will work with you to validate your hunches and improve your intuition.

Walk with Your Angel

In the descriptions above, you may have noticed that most of them have an affinity with nature, so communing with them outside is a great way to connect. Open your mind and heart and chat with them as you walk. You can speak out loud or communicate using your thoughts, whatever makes you feel comfortable. Depending on the angels who reply, you will receive messages and synchronicities of their presence to signal they are listening.

Meditate with Your Angel

Meditation is the perfect state of mind for communicating with your angels because you're calm, receptive, and focused. Choose a calm place to meditate and light a single white candle. Sit comfortably and take deep breaths as you clear your mind. Feel yourself slowing your thoughts and invite your angels to communicate with you.

Create a Specific Time for Your Communication

We all know the power of an organized life with a time for work and leisure. Working to a schedule works for most people, and the angels recognize the benefits of an organized mind. Set aside five minutes of your day to meditate and talk to your angels. You can start or finish your day with this time for connection, so you maintain regular contact. Don't forget that you can always contact your angel when you need them, but this regular contact signifies that you're committed and constant.

Signs Your Angels Are There for You

When you're given messages from the Heavens, it will affect your emotions and feelings, but they will also manifest in certain physical forms. Watch out for these angelic signs of their presence:

- **Animals**

When you see animals and birds, do you get an overwhelming feeling of wonder? A bird or an animal who seems to be focused on you and makes you feel special could signify that your angel is sending you a sign. Butterflies and robins will often be sent to comfort you when grieving a loved one.

- **Rainbows**

Seeing this glorious natural phenomenon can raise your spirits, and angels will often send them to make you feel their love. The colors and shape of a rainbow inspire love and happiness and will make you aware of nature's glory.

- **Coins**

Celestial beings love shiny coins of small value. They will place them in unusual places for you to find, so you're reminded of their presence. Always pick up a stray coin and keep it with you; it is a symbolic gift of leadership and support from your angel.

- **Goosebumps**

When the temperature changes without any obvious cause, the feeling you get is a sure sign you're in angelic company. Tingling at the back of your neck or goosebumps on your arm are clear signs they are watching over you. Don't be afraid; the sign is meant to comfort you, so don't be alarmed at a sudden temperature change.

- **Dreams**

When we sleep, our minds are rested and receptive to messages. Always keep a journal and pen by your bed so you can record any nighttime dreams and recollections that may be significant. Angels will often inhabit your dreams and use their powers to guide you or send you advice.

- **Feathers**

One of the more well-known angelic signs is feathers. White ones signal your angel's presence, and colored ones are sent to convey more complex messages.

What Colored Feathers Mean

- **Pink feathers** mean unconditional love. If the feather appears while you're thinking about someone, the angels are telling you that love is in the air. Angels send pink feathers to show their love for you and remind you they are there for you.
- **Red feathers** signal health and rejuvenation. If you have had health issues, red feathers are sent to tell you that you're on the right path to healthier times. If they are deep red, it is a sign that passion is about to enter your life, so prepare yourself for some heat.
- **Orange feathers** are a signal that you need to be more spontaneous and have more fun. Take a look at your life and remember how it feels to let go and find new ways to be more creative. Let the flow of life take you to new places and give yourself a chance to grow.
- **Yellow feathers** are sent to signal that you're on the right path to success. If you have asked your angels for advice about a project, they will send yellow feathers to tell you to go for it.
- **Green feathers** are sent to tell you that money or abundance is in your future. It is also a gentle reminder to take better care of yourself and check your health. Green feathers are sent to nurture

you and show support from the angels.

• **Blue feathers** signify your angel is sending healing energy to regenerate your physical self. It is a sign that your divine connections are strong, and the universe supports your choices.

• **Gray feathers** signify peace. When you're experiencing mental turmoil or stress, it is a reminder to center yourself and be aware that your situation is never as hopeless as it seems. The angels are showing you that they are working to help you overcome your challenges and move forward.

• **Brown feathers** signify the connection between the physical world and your energy levels. They remind you to seek solace in nature and maintain a balanced perspective.

• **Black feathers** are sent when you need reassurance and support. You may be experiencing grief or sadness, and the angels are showing you how to recover from your dark emotions.

Chapter 3: How to Use Angelic Sigils

Think about how important your signature is. You use it to make documents official, make bank transfers, sign contracts, seal deals, and countless other times. It is your stamp on the world and should be your mark that others cannot use or violate. Angelic sigils are an angel's signature and should be used with the same reverence you use your signature. They are your gift from the Heavens so treat them with respect and love.

Angelic Sigil Rituals

The Candle Ritual

Your first step is to choose the angel you want to summon and create a representation of their sigil. Trace the symbol onto a piece of paper or print it from an online source. If you prefer a more personal connection, you can draw the sigil freehand onto a piece of paper. This gives you a heightened connection with your chosen angel and signals your intention.

Clear a space and create an altar or sacred place to perform your ritual. Add elements that are associated with your angel. For instance, if you're attracting Raphael, add a feather, a windchime, or another item connected to the air element. For Michael, add a candle or a lamp to represent fire. For Gabriel, add liquid, a bowl of water, or a chalice filled with wine for the element water. The element of the earth represents Uriel, so add natural soil or dirt to your altar.

Place your sigil on the altar and surround it with three white candles. Place your favorite crystals and gemstones around the edge of the sigil to signal your intent. Shut off all other light sources and let the candlelight fill your senses. As you gaze at the candles, ask for the archangel of your choice to join you and see the light.

As you gaze, the sigil may appear to float away from the paper and hover in the air. You may hear strange sounds like gentle singing or a low humming. This signifies that the energy in the room has altered, and a higher force has joined you. Keep your breathing calm and steady, and focus on the sigil and how it appears to you. At this point, you can repeat your chosen angel's name in a low voice and wait for an audial sign your angel is close. They may repeat their name after you have said it, or they may say your name. Whatever happens, accept the process, and embrace the love.

The Mantra Ritual

Not everybody has the resources to create an altar at will, but they still want to use sigils to attract attention from the Heavens. All you need for this ritual is a quiet place and a marker pen. Choose the angel you want to interact with and what their sigil looks like. Take the marker pen and copy the sigil onto the back of your right hand. Sit comfortably in your quiet space and hold the back of your right hand to your forehead as you chant the angel's name while focusing on their energy.

If your environment is suitable, raise the volume of your voice as the mantra continues. Every name has a different energy, and the vibrational energy you create will stay with you for days. When you chant a mantra, you surround yourself with joyful energy, and your emotional and physical state is elevated. There are always simple ways to perform rituals, and this one doesn't need tools or fancy settings. All you need is intention and energy.

Contemplate an Angel

Angels are well documented, and the more you know about them, the deeper your understanding of them becomes. This is especially relevant when summoning a lesser-known angel, like Sandalphon. Read texts and articles about him and get to know your angel like you would know a new friend. When we meet people in real life, we connect via social media, and we check out what we have in common and our mutual interests and friends. Do the same with your angel and get to know more about them.

For instance, here are some interesting facts about Sandalphon.

- He is one of the two archangels who originally lived on Earth. His mortal form was as the Prophet Elijah, and he transcended to Heaven after his mortal life was over.
- He is the tallest of the angels, and Moses reported his height after seeing and meeting Sandalphon in the third Heaven.
- He works well with Metatron, a mortal, and transcended to heaven after living as the first Prophet Enoch.
- He has an aura that resonates with nature. Brown earth hues and blue skies with bright sunlight form part of his energy. He loves to communicate with outdoorsy types and can easily tune into their vibrational fields.
- He is the archangel responsible for the pregnancy and helps expectant mothers through the process. He is responsible for the unborn child's safety and watches over their souls if they die during pregnancy.
- He helps you to find people of your wavelength. When you move or change jobs, connecting with already-established people can be difficult. Ask Sandalphon for advice about people who have the same aura spectrum as you so that you can form relationships with compatible beings.

Use Your Sigil to Connect to Sandalphon

Now you know more about Sandalphon, you realize he works better outdoors. Choose a place of natural beauty like a lake or forest and create an area to meditate. Lay a piece of paper with his sigil on the floor and take deep breaths as you invoke his presence and ask him to guide you. Imagine your spiritual energy emitting from the top of your head and joining the force of nature as you connect to this mighty angel.

Repeat the mantra: "I call on thee, Sandalphon, to send me your energy. Your sigil will be my chosen symbol when I feel the need for your energy and love. Fill my heart and mind with the strength of your creativity and make me more adventurous and courageous. Heal my emotional scars and help me emerge as a well-rounded friend to those who need me. Stand by my side as I travel my path and hold my heart in your hands as you accompany me."

Prayers to the Major Archangels

One of the most interesting facts about working with celestial beings and spiritual entities is they love to form a team. We all know the power of joining a group and creating a buzz about projects. Angels are just the same; they bring more to the table when they work together. Reaching out to the more widely known archangels will ensure you have a great team leader who will know exactly whom to get on board to help you become more evolved and spiritually enlightened.

Never forget we are all part of the One, and we share the universe with all beings on all planes; when you pray, your prayers are not just for yourself but for the good of mankind. Work as a collective and feel the force of their angelic inspirations and strength.

Prayer 1 for Archangel Michael

"I appeal to the might of the Archangel Michael and all his legions.

Remove any negative energy and harmful influences from my soul, mind, heart, and home.

Help me live with a deep love in my heart that takes me to the right path for my enlightenment.

Help my family and friends overcome their obstacles and live in harmony with the universe.

Guide us to the ultimate light and bathe us in its glow.

Be my inspiration and help me fight the darkness within and cast it out.

Make me successful and productive in my career and motivate me to do better.

Vanquish my nightmares and fill my dreams with positivity and love.

Thank you, Amen."

Prayer 2 for Archangel Raphael

"I send my prayers to Raphael and the legion of healing angels to make me whole in mind, body, and spirit.

Bring healing energy to my family and friends and help them live a pure, whole life on all dimensions and planes.

Alleviate our emotional wounds and help us learn from them so we can live a better life in this incarnation and the next.

Bring us peace and harmony to help other people heal and live better lives to create universal harmony and joy.

Bring abundance into my life and help me become a healer of men.

I ask for his assistance on my travels and implore him to look over me as I embark on my spiritual and physical journeys.

Clear my heart of negativity and fill it with your healing kindness as I strive to share my abundance with others.

Thank you, Amen."

Prayer 3 for Archangel Gabriel

"I call upon the angel Gabriel and his legion of mighty messengers to guide my family and me to the right path.

Send us messages, counsel us when we ask for help, and direct us towards the light.

Show us the way to communicate with higher beings and become enlightened with their wisdom.

Be our strength in times of sorrow and give us hope when we feel defeated and down.

Help me forgive those that have harmed me and brought sorrow into my life.

Give me the strength to grant them mercy and help them to see the error of their deeds.

Help others forgive me if I have done wrong to them and welcome me back into their lives.

When I face a temptation to take the wrong path, guide me with your heavenly might back to the path of righteousness.

Help me show benevolence and forgiveness to all and fill my heart with love.

Thank you, Amen."

Prayer 4 for Archangel Jophiel

"I appeal to the Archangel Jophiel to bring her natural joy and love into my life.

Give me the insight into how to live a lighter life filled with love and laughter so I can experience the lightness of heart her energy generates.

Bring your loving energy into the lives of the people who surround me and keep us safe from negativity.

Shield us with your love and purity so we can be safe and filled with your jubilation and elation.

Bring us the inspiration to be more creative and boost our imagination so we can achieve new goals.

Allow me to appreciate the beauty that surrounds me and fill my mind with beautiful thoughts.

Help us all to realize our potential, break free of barriers that stand in our way, and help us see life clearly and all its details.

Thank you, Amen."

Prayer 5 for Archangel Metatron

"My prayers are directed to the mighty Archangel Metatron to give me the knowledge to connect my spiritual being with my physical self.

Share your strength with my closest friends to become a team for good on Earth.

Channel the love of God into our lives and let us feel his power and protection.

Bless our lives with your highest energy and your angelic protection.

Provide me with answers when I am lost to negotiate life's path.

Give us the strength to make changes and guide us to the right decisions as we grow and become enlightened.

Thank you, Amen."

Prayer 6 for Archangel Chamuel

"My prayers are for Chamuel, the angel of harmony.

I ask for his strength to create harmony and peace wherever I am.

Connect me with nature and let me share the bounty of the Earth so I can become part of the universal family of love.

Help me find my true self and encourage others to find their inner peace with trust and love.

Show me how we all connect and what I need to do to strengthen those connections.

Open my heart to the love that others show me and help me learn to appreciate them.

Clear my mind of toxic thoughts and protect me from negative energy when I feel attached.

Thank you, Amen."

Prayer 7 for Archangel Azrael

"My heart and soul appeal to the power of Azrael to help me find comfort when loved ones pass.

Help me understand the natural passage of time and the cycle of life.

Make me strong for others and give me the power to comfort them in dark times.

Help us cross the void between life and death and connect with our ancestors and those who have gone before us.

Stand by me when I feel alone and give me the strength to heal my heart.

Thank you, Amen."

Don't worry if you don't know which angel to choose; they know your needs and how to help. As you pray, focus on the sigils of the Archangels, and your heart will be open to their messages. They will be a part of your life, providing you have pure intentions and live a good life.

Angels

Archangels and their counterparts are considered some of the most powerful beings in the spiritual world and are often called upon for their assistance. Some religions describe angels as the heavenly representation of the word of God. It is impossible to list every angel who lives in the realms, and one quote suggests there are "myriads of myriads and thousands of thousands of angels." This doesn't mean there are 100 million angels. It simply means it is impossible to estimate.

We know that they form a heavenly hierarchy and are all individuals who have a connection with God. They will never interfere with your free will, but they can give advice and assistance. Archangels act as the principles in school. They govern the heavens and designate earthly duties to their legions of angels who serve them. They guide the world we live in (from the simplest being to governments), and they oversee countries and continents as part of their duties.

Regular angels walk among us and are part of our society. They visit regularly and then report back to heaven. They aren't censorious, just concerned with our spiritual and physical well-being. When you live well and follow a moral code, they recognize your devotion and reward you.

Make good use of the sigils by creating jewelry or artwork based on the shape. Placing symbols and sigils around your physical form will help you remain connected even when doing the most mundane tasks. Cosmic energy is a powerful force that keeps you alive. As a form of cosmic energy, every part of the universe has a lively vibration of pure energy that binds us all, from the smallest atom to the highest beings.

When you're born, you emerge from the womb as a speck of cosmic energy, a seed of the Higher Being, and you begin to grow. Cosmic energy gives you the strength to advance and evolve, and surrounding yourself with positive symbols and sigils keeps your energy channels free from negativity. Avoid unhealthy energy sources like junk food and alcohol so you can be more receptive to the cosmic force. Inhale the positive energy of the angels and become interwoven with their force. Regardless of your religious beliefs or cultural teachings, the angels are part of human heritage and are available to all.

Chapter 4: Astrological Glyphs

The heavens and the universe are vast areas containing the mysteries of man and how they connect with the beings that watch over them. The stars and planets that populate that area are a complex blueprint of that fact and contain clues that reveal the nature of mankind in all its hues and shades. Every sign associated with the twelve zodiac signs depicts man's evolution. When we learn how to read and understand them, we get a deeper insight into the psyche of the universe.

The zodiac belt that contains the Earth is divided into twelve sections of thirty degrees. It begins with Aries, the representation of the head and new existences, and finishes with Pisces, the representation of the feet and the cessation of the current form. The signs found in the belt have evolved over time – but still represent the essential meanings they originally stood for. The twelve zodiac signs are represented by glyphs that are purposeful marks consisting of a single image or symbol.

The Zodiac Wheel

Aries

The Aries glyph is symbolic of a fountain with two curved arms gushing into the air. It is also known as the fountain of Life, and it embodies the burst of youthful energy that signals the beginning of the astrological year. Some people see the glyph as a new seed shooting through the earth and bringing abundance to the world. It is also described as a representation of the human face with eyebrows and a nose, suggesting man's rebirth. The image also resembles the horns of the ram, an animal that rules the sign and gives a feeling of male potency and the instinctive need to survive.

Taurus

This glyph resembles its animal ruler, a circle topped by a pair of horns in the form of a crescent moon. The bull is a steadfast creature associated with passion, strength, and a stubborn refusal to change paths. Despite its masculine overtones, the glyph has definite femininity, with the circle and crescent moon being powerful feminine symbols, but as they are displayed, the overall feeling is masculine strength and stability.

Gemini

This glyph represents the duality of the sign. The mercurial personality of man combined with the need for duality and a feeling of universal wholeness emanates from the two straight lines with crescent moons at the base and the top. According to ancient legends, the glyph is a depiction of the twins, Castor and Pollux, woven into the constellation and standing at the gates of heaven. It also resembles Roman number two, which strengthens the union between matter and spirit. An epicene nature, neither male nor female, indicates a path to knowledge.

Cancer

The glyph for this zodiac sign represents two claws, signifying the crab that rules the sign. The other definition is the two female breasts which are the source of nutrition for all life. In the past, the scarab beetle has represented the sign, an Egyptian symbol meaning eternal life and the belief that man lives long after his demise on Earth. The curved image suggests the mathematical symbol for infinity and suggests that the outer curved surface protects the soft underbelly of the glyph. This strength and vulnerability are qualities associated with Cancerians, combined with their mercurial links to the cycles of the Moon.

Leo

This glyph represents the *king of the jungle* with a flowing mane emanating from a solid head. The dramatic flow of the symbol suggests passion and creativity intertwined with a sense of pride and high self-esteem. Leo represents the magnitude of mankind and how they can take their lead from people in power and emulate their vitality. The sense of life force is strong, and it projects hope and warmth with its positive energy. Leos are sensitive but know how to hide their vulnerability with a dignified stance.

Virgo

This decorative glyph is based on the Hebrew letter "Mem," attributed to deeply feminine traits. The symbol of the M with an added tail suggests closed-off energy protected by angelic wings, which indicates purity and fidelity. Virgos often perform selfless acts and are willing to dedicate themselves to worthwhile causes to make the world a better place without any thought for their wellbeing. They create an ordered existence even in the most chaotic circumstances and are renowned for their sense of calm.

Libra

A straight line with a setting sun about to disappear over the horizon is the glyph for Libra. It indicates the balance of power between the day and night, giving the impression of mediation and harmony. Librans are accomplished social beings and will strive to bring cohesion and unity to their social circle. They tend to neglect their own needs to bring balance to others. They are the scales that weigh all the options and make the right decision when called upon to mediate.

Scorpio

This glyph is like Virgo with its Hebrew letter "Mem" but with an added sting in the tail. It is indicative of the scorpion and the deadly barb that lies on the end of its tail. Scorpions are proud animals who will sting themselves to death rather than be defeated by another creature. Scorpions are the signs that are most likely to transform themselves and pursue their ambitions with passionate energy. They have the power of endurance that pushes them to achieve their highest potential and become their best selves.

Sagittarius

The glyph for Sagittarius is an arrow emitting from a cross pointing heavenwards. It inspires the psyche and pushes man to achieve the unachievable. The symbol represents freedom of choice and the pace needed for expansion. The glyph encourages reaching for the stars and removing limits or barriers that can stand in the way. It is filled with optimism and emphasizes the connection between us on earth and the higher planes. Sagittarians are, by nature, individuals who think beyond standard concepts and have an intuitive sense of when to challenge the rules. They are the messengers of man and will spread their gospel of enthusiasm and hope as far as the eye can see. Their enthusiasm for learning is infectious, and they can often be found in teaching roles and positions.

Capricorn

This is the most complex glyph with a V sign attached to a goat's head with curled horns. Some people believe it is a combination of two separate glyphs, emphasizing the Capricorns need for confusion and anonymity. They don't like to share their personal details with people, which gives them a sense of being cold and distant. In reality, they are guarded and organized because they are ambitious and focused on self-achievement. Capricorns know that if they are seen as vulnerable, they will be distracted by social issues and lose focus on their financial and social goals.

Aquarius

The two electric bolts that form the glyph for Aquarius represent knowledge. The waves they form indicate a crackling outpouring of wisdom from the higher planes and how it affects mankind. Aquarians are dedicated to bringing freedom to humans and creating an idyll for them to live in. The traditional symbol for Aquarius is a man pouring a pitcher of water into the ground and making it bring forth life. Their innovative and free-thinking approach to life brings people together and creates a brotherhood that spans continents and borders.

Pisces

The glyph for Pisces is two semi-circles bound by a crossbar. The bar creates a clear indication of separation between two worlds, heaven and earth, and creates a cord that joins the two existences. The astrological sign for Pisces is two fish swimming in opposite directions representing the contrasting experiences of the creative and stoic being, the savior and victim, and reality and make-believe. Some Pisceans follow their creative and mystical side, while others remain down to earth and invest in their worldly self.

Planetary Glyphs

These glyphs and symbols show us a more practical look at the planet's influence on our lives. Initially, alchemists collaborated to create the science of astrology and assigned combinations of alchemic symbols to represent the energy of the astral bodies and how they play a part in the cosmic weave. These glyphs and symbols have been used throughout history, and well-respected astrologers have used them to improve insight into what the respective planets mean to each of us.

These Glyphs Are All Created from Four Basic Shapes

The circle: the ultimate spirit, and vitality. The creator of life and giver of energy.

The crescent: when facing upwards, it is aligned with the superconscious, and when it is facing down, it represents the perceptions we receive via our subconscious. Facing right or left signifies the connection to the left and right sides of the human brain. The left side controls most basic functions like speech and language. It is responsible for rational decision-making and verbal sequences. The right side is the brain's creative side, responsible for non-verbal communications and intuition. The right hemisphere processes spatial awareness and random thoughts.

The cross represents the more pragmatic aspect of human existence and focuses on practical matters.

The arrow signifies energy and direction. It focuses the mind on specific aims and shows which way to succeed.

Colors also play an integral part in these glyphs and correlate with the energies they produce. They are chosen to correspond with the light reflected from their surfaces as seen from Earth.

Sun

The source of life for the galaxy, its glyph is a solid red dot in a larger red circle on a yellow background. The dot indicates the central position of the sun and the power of its position. In individuals, this can be seen as arrogance but is more likely to be assertiveness and self-confidence that originates from having the courage to believe in yourself.

Moon

A red left-facing crescent on a white background, the white represents the purity of the moon and the cleansing properties its energy brings. The left-facing crescent is a sign of the practical properties of this important satellite as it keeps our planet illuminated as the sun disappears.

Mercury

A black upward-facing crescent is topping a circle resting on a cross on a dark pink background. The crescent represents the connection to an awareness that supersedes both the conscious and subconscious mind. The cross indicates a link to the primeval sense of materialism and abundance, while the circle creates an area of peace between the two heightened states. Mercury brings an energy that encourages interrelation between our intellect and the superconscious part of the mind.

Venus

A black circle resting on a cross surrounded by a deep red background, the glyph is indicative of the distance between Venus and the Sun. It resembles a handheld mirror that suggests that Venus is the energy that encourages us to reflect on ourselves and find ways to improve. It gives us the confidence to find common values in others and balance the spirit to create harmonious existences.

Earth

There are two glyphs used to represent Earth, and the least common one is the inverted glyph of Venus. This is because the planets are similar in size and dimension, and their energies work well together. The more familiar glyph of the cross enclosed in a circle with a dark brown background indicates the base element of our terrestrial lives firmly implanted on solid ground.

Mars

This is a black circle with an arrow pointing to the right side of the area on an orange background. The energy of the circle indicates man's willpower, and the arrow suggests a force of dynamism that pushes them to achieve greatness. Mars is the driving force behind confidence and balance that allows us to evolve and improve.

Jupiter

This glyph is a black left-facing crescent with an attached cross of matter on a blue background. It is a balanced representation of spiritual ambition and materialistic expectations. When we focus on the crescent, we feel the need to explore and be adventurous even when it may be hazardous to do so. The cross brings our attention back to earth and grounds us to harness our explorations, so we continue to consider other people's feelings. Jupiter is a plateau from which we can explore and return to normality.

Saturn

A black cross with an inverted crescent set in a sage green background shows maturity and a deep connection with man's heritage. The downward crescent shows a tendency to become overwhelmed by past mistakes and a fear of progress, while the cross reminds us to keep our thoughts on practical matters. Saturn isn't the most explosive energy source, but it is a stark reminder that sometimes we need to function in society and become part of a responsible collective.

Uranus

A complex glyph of the cross of matter flanked by two outward-facing crescents topping a circle on a lilac background indicates the energy of Uranus. It appears in flashes and peaks like a radio signal that attracts other frequencies from near and far. Uranus also has an arrow on top of the Sun glyph, which marries the conscious mind with the superconscious form of thinking. Uranus is a powerful energy and uses grounded symbols to prevent explosive waves from overwhelming our considerations. It allows us to bring new ideas to the table and be bold and innovative.

Neptune

A black upward crescent is laid over an inverted cross of matter on a bright blue background; this glyph is concentrated on understanding some of the more complex superconscious myths and applying them to practical matters. The cross helps us deal with disappointments when some of our more outlandish efforts fail, giving us the confidence to start again. The European version of the glyph replaces the cross with a circle for a more dynamic representation leaving three distinct lines all pointing upwards with a positive thrusting motion.

Pluto

This plucky little planet has four glyphs that include a circle atop a full crescent, a circle in an upturned crescent over a small cross, a left-facing crescent against a straight line to form a P shape, and a fountain shape on a circle. A purple background surrounds all the glyphs. The variations indicate a conflicting mix of energies battling to become Pluto's purpose. They range from transformation to practical and can change things up.

Other Astrological Terms

Hades

A right-facing crescent covers a cross of matter on a dark purple background. The planet of the underworld, according to Greek mythology, is a deep, dank place where the karmic threads of past lives can be found. They reflect the fears and anxieties we bring with us from past lives and give us the chance to resolve them. Hades may seem like a dark place, but it also offers hope and the opportunity to heal. The cross represents the collective subconscious, and the crescent suggests that intuition and communication are the best solutions for past life resolutions.

Zeus

The glyph is an arrow rising from the center of four open bottom triangles (or a tilted cross) on a purple background. Zeus in astrology is the planet of channeling and intelligence. The glyph is a powerful symbol of fertility and new life with controlled directives and leadership.

Kronos

A dark cross topped by a downward crescent on a light purple background, Kronos is the planet of authority and power. Governments and leaders benefit from the energy of Kronos and on the other end of the spectrum, so do despots and successful criminals. The crescent indicates the protection of those under your authority, and people born under this planetary energy will be natural leaders who rule with an iron fist.

Apollon

The glyph is complex, with three crescents connected by straight lines on an orange background. The crescents represent the three states of consciousness and perceptions arising from the brain's superconscious, subconscious, and intuitive areas. Apollon is the planet of wisdom and the balance of past and present experiences. It is a planet with balanced energies with the ability to act quickly and then regain calm when needed.

Admetos

The cross of the matter is topped with an upward crescent and encompassed in a circle on dark blue background. It is the planet of blocked energy and transformative power, and if it features in your birth chart, it indicates solidity and weight.

Vulkanus

A triangle topped by an arrow on a blue background, the glyph is a powerful indication of channeling higher powers. It has athletic energy with brute force and potential, but it can become dangerous and capable of brutality when it is vulnerable. It can produce increased determination bordering on the obsessive when it aligns with the sun.

Poseidon

An upward crescent and a downward crescent are joined by a vertical bar on a pale purple background; this glyph symbolizes a higher spiritual understanding married with a deep-seated connection with the earth. Planet Poseidon is filled with understanding of the past, present, and future, providing an overall view of the collective we all belong to.

Chapter 5: Totem Animals

As you begin to explore the symbolism of animals and their importance in your life, you will find the meanings behind their presence and an insight into the wisdom and spirituality they bring to your life. Totem animals are also referred to as spirit animals and soulmate animals. These animals include land animals, water animals, crustaceans, birds, and insects. They shouldn't be confused with Native Indian beliefs, which concentrate on animals indigenous to their home.

They will stay with you for life and guide you through your journey. Totem animals are spiritual energies that will bring balance to your life and make sure you choose the right path. All aspects of your life benefit from their protection; these amazing spirits will boost your spiritual, physical, and emotional strength. Sometimes you will need their strength, and at other times you may need their compassion and love. This is why you have a team in place; they all have characteristics you will need at some point.

The first thing to realize is you don't choose your totem animals; they choose you. There can be as many as nine animals forming your spiritual animal team, where the term totem originates. There are too many totem animals, but the list below gives you a fairly comprehensive idea of the most common animals people are drawn to and what they signify.

How to Recognize Your Totem Animals

Your instincts will help you recognize your totem animals. They are familiar to you, and you already recognize them as part of your life. Do you see butterflies even on the coldest days? Are you mad about dogs or cats? Do you have a particular animal you regularly watch documentaries about or dream of? If you see particular animals regularly, they may be part of your animal totem team.

If you dream of these animals, pay attention to where they appear or how you feel when you see them. It is believed the nine animals represent the four cardinal points of North, East, West, and South, above and below you, within you, and the final two animals walk by your side.

What the Position of Your Animal Means

- **North**: Encourages us to be thankful and mindful of our communications
- **South:** The guardian of your inner child
- **West:** Gives you the strength of self-confidence
- **East:** Deals with your spiritual growth and challenges
- **Above:** Your dream guardian who protects you from evil
- **Below:** Clears obstacles from your path and keeps you grounded
- **Within:** Guardian of your soul and makes sure you're happy
- **Walk to the Right:** Protects and nurtures your masculine characteristics
- **Walks to the Left:** Protects and nurtures your feminine characteristics

List of Totem Animals and Their Meanings

Remember, thousands of animals may appear on your horizon, so don't worry if not all your totem animals are included; it just means you have attracted more unique spirit animals.

- **Alligator:** Amazing survival skills, strong maternal instincts, and swift to move
- **Ant**: Works well in a group and is resolute and productive
- **Armadillo**: Steadfast, prefers their own company and is trustful
- **Bat:** Attentive, keeps secrets, longevity
- **Bear:** Immense power, subliminal wisdom, bravery
- **Bee:** Productive, loyal, part of a team
- **Bull:** Impulsive, fertile, raw power
- **Butterfly:** Transfiguration, symmetry, natural grace
- **Caribou:** Reliability, leadership, compassion
- **Cheetah**: Fast-moving, clear intentions, forward-thinking
- **Cow:** Patience, calm nature, happiness
- **Cobra:** Duplicitous, energetic, quixotic
- **Crane**: Long life, mediation, seclusion
- **Crow:** Transformation, creativity, strong spiritual strength
- **Deer:** Empathy, calm, wisdom
- **Dog:** Faithful, protection, guidance
- **Dolphin:** Emotional depth, mischievous, joy
- **Dove:** Serenity, love, peace
- **Dragon:** Wealth, intelligence, strength
- **Eagle:** Freedom, healing powers, inventive
- **Elephant:** Intelligence, family orientated, faithful
- **Elk:** Power, steadfastness, self-confidence
- **Falcon:** Adventurous, committed, new starts
- **Flamingo:** Playful, sociable, adaptable
- **Fox:** Cunning, swift, agile
- **Gazelle:** Natural beauty, cognizance, drive
- **Giraffe:** Wisdom, stature, beauty
- **Gorilla:** Leadership, protection, focused

- **Grasshopper:** Fast thinking, lucky, high moral standards
- **Hawk:** Nobility, success, restorative powers
- **Hippopotamus:** Deep-seated emotions, family values, strength
- **Horse:** Grace, forward-thinking, strength
- **Hummingbird:** Ageless, healing, savior
- **Jaguar:** Self-confidence, bravery, chaotic energy
- **Lion:** Regality, pride, family
- **Lizard:** Self-survival, wisdom, hidden depths
- **Llama:** Compassion, steadfastness, leadership qualities
- **Moose:** Instinctive, ageless, impulsive
- **Octopus:** Nocturnal instincts, wisdom, survival
- **Opossum:** Quick-witted, practical, sensible
- **Otter:** Energetic, childlike, welcoming
- **Owl:** Wisdom, far-sighted, quixotic
- **Panther:** Adaptable, protective, sensible
- **Peacock:** Heightened sense of self-importance, pride, longevity
- **Penguin:** Teamwork, discipline, a sense of purpose
- **Quail:** Works well with others, leadership, bravery
- **Rabbit:** Fertile, creative, happiness
- **Rat:** Scavenger, quick-witted, ambitious
- **Raven:** Otherworldly, self-aware, magical
- **Salmon:** Rebirth, driven, focused
- **Scorpion:** Disorganized, strong, inspirational
- **Snake:** Sheds layers, shrewd, adventurous
- **Tiger:** Bravery, strength, power
- **Turtle:** Shyness, strength, family values
- **Weasel:** Clever, stealthy, untamed
- **Whale:** Adventurer, self-awareness, loyalty
- **Wolf:** Faithful, enduring, success

How Your Totem Animal May Be Associated with Your Zodiac Sign

We are all aware of the importance of the cosmic effect on our birthday and how it influences the rest of our lives. It would be foolish to think that didn't impact our totem animals as well. Our signs accurately depict our characteristics and personality traits, which means that certain animals will be drawn to people born under different Zodiac signs. Of course, everyone knows some people fit these traits better than others; we all have a friend who is a "typical … (insert Zodiac sign) because she does (insert trait). Discovering your totem animal gives you a deep insight into yourself and teaches important lessons about life. The animal connected to your Zodiac sign may not be the most prominent animal on your team, but it will be the "ride or die" animal who will be there for you when you need it most.

Aries Totem Animal Is the Cheetah

Just like the cheetah, you're constantly on the go, and you need an outlet for your energy. The speed and force of your nature drive you to success, and you're a natural leader who also loves to lead from the front. Sometimes your instincts will make you break away and discover your path alone.

Because you're hyper-focused, you rarely fail. Once you set your mind to achieve something, it is a done deal. The force of your personality drives you to success, and you can dedicate all your energy to your goals. The downside of this is you can become self-obsessed and ignore the needs of others.

Just like the cheetah, you can be brutal and aggressive when needed. This may manifest as hot-headedness and mercurial mood swings that can be disturbing. You also share your opinion with utmost honesty, which can be a bit brutal. This tendency can upset people without meaning to, but your passion for life leads to outbursts of honesty straight from your heart.

The cheetah represents your fiery personality and lightning mood changes, but you're spontaneous when it comes to dating. Your partner needs to be as on board with you as you're with them. Casual doesn't work for you; if you're giving up your single status, it needs to be with a partner that is fully committed.

Taurus Totem Animal Is the Bear

When a bear plants its paws on the ground and reaches for the sky, they fill the area with strength and stability. Nobody would attempt to move them or interfere with their environment, which relates to Taurus individuals. They are the rock their family and friends need, and they believe in setting down roots. Bears protect their young with a palpable ferocity, and you're the same. You would protect your family with your life.

Taureans are a creature of habit and rarely welcome change. They love a balanced life filled with quality and will work hard to achieve their comfortable existence. Patience isn't just a virtue for them. They are one of the most mellow signs of the zodiac, but the protective nature of the bear is just below the surface, and they will get frustrated eventually.

Just like the bear, Taureans don't believe in wasting energy. This can be perceived as lazy, but they have no interest in menial tasks and prefer to save their energy for more worthwhile pursuits. This means if you date a Taurus, you will have to assume the slack in the home – or the household duties will be overlooked. The upside is that Taureans are physically active when it comes to sex and will always find the energy for physical interactions.

Gemini Totem Animal Is the Dolphin

Dolphins will often do things purely for fun, and Gemini is just as curious and playful. They focus more on pleasurable activities and can neglect their careers to focus on their social life and traveling. Their dual personality can be mercurial and indecisive, but they are eternally optimistic, just like their totem animal, and always seem to be living life to the fullest.

Forming social groups is important to Geminis, and they love their friends passionately. They include them in activities and encourage them to bloom. Geminis in relationships can be frustrating as they tend to move on quickly when they get bored. You need to keep it fun and energetic to hold onto a Gemini, so they aren't tempted to look elsewhere.

Dolphins love to learn tricks and perform in front of others, and Gemini individuals are also born performers. They light up a room and can talk to anyone.

Cancer Totem Animal Is the Rabbit

Like the rabbit, Cancerians aren't good at mixing with people they don't know. They appear timid and shy but are always thinking and calculating how to overcome difficulties. Naturally inquisitive and curious rabbits are braver than they look and hide behind a cute and fluffy exterior. Cancers love hard, and they love long. Treat them right, and they are the most loyal partners who always have your back.

Leo Totem Animal Is the Dragon

When you picture a dragon, they are generally ready for action. Legs up, breathing fire, and making an impact on those around them, Leos are just the same. They love to lead and use their powerful personalities to pave the way for others. Showing off to other people and proving themselves as skilled creatures is high on their list of personality traits, and they are often perceived as arrogant.

Leos are often accused of being overly dramatic, but their passion is sometimes mistaken for drama. They aren't prone to gossip, and if they have something to say, they will state their case honestly. They don't wear their emotions on their sleeve, which makes them seem cold and unapproachable, but they genuinely love people, especially those close to them. Leos are ambitious and driven and can be perceived as aloof, but they are loyal and loving once you get to know them.

Virgo Totem Animal Is the Fox

Not the biggest member of the canine family, foxes are seen as sly and devious when they are intelligent and smart in reality. They may be small, but their mind power makes up for their lack of stature. Virgos are mentally strong and have an innate ability to make even the most uncomfortable place feel like home. Natural homemakers and nurturers, Virgos can adapt to new situations and surroundings. They match well with other Earth signs and grounded individuals. A partnership with a Virgo will last, providing you respect their privacy and share their goal-orientated work ethic. It won't be the most passionate relationship, but you will be loved.

Libra Totem Animal Is the Swan

Elegant and graceful, a swan seems to glide across the water. As Librans, you have a natural grace that makes it seem like you belong wherever you're. Even though there is a beautiful soft exterior, the whole ethos of the swan is based on strength. They are powerful birds who can defeat the strongest predators with just one kick.

They find balance in troubled times and are great mediators. In relationships, they prefer peaceful and romantic couplings, and they love to be in love. They can be needy and will do anything for a person they love, which makes them seem weak, but they are eager to please and see it as romantic when they do things for their partner. They are intensely monogamous and will never cheat or be unfaithful.

Scorpio Totem Animal Is the Phoenix

Scorpios rise into the firmament like the phoenix and create a spectacular display. They do this to protect their vulnerable side because they figure you won't realize they have a softer side if you're distracted by their flamboyance. Symbolizing the ultimate rebirth, Scorpios are adept at changing and are brave enough to take alternative routes.

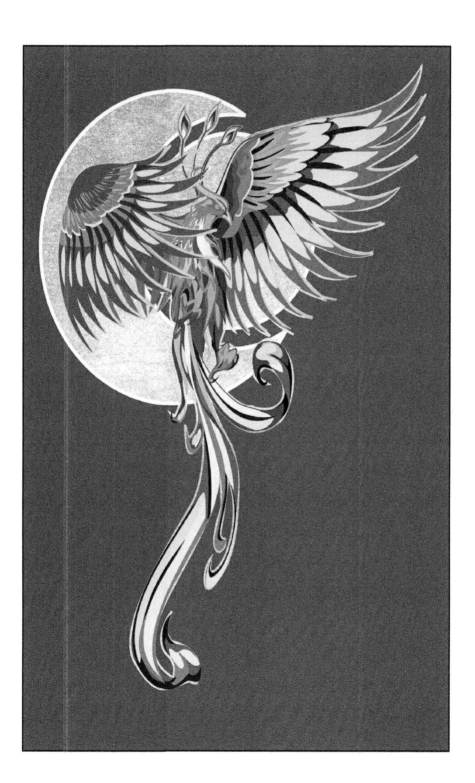

In relationships, they are passionate and loyal but can be jealous. They are intense, and they can often misinterpret friendship as potential cheating. Because of this trait, they can be controlling and ask too much of their partners when it comes to being together; they expect them to be always available. If anybody dares to say no to a Scorpio, they will suffer the consequences and quickly witness their tendency to anger.

Sagittarius Totem Animal Is the Cat

Anybody who has ever owned a cat knows you don't own your pet; they just choose to live with you – for now. Sagittarians are the same; you can't tie them down or locate them; they will march to their drumbeat no matter what. They are quite happy alone, especially when traveling, because this means they can go wherever they like without having to consult someone else.

They are very social and love company. Their natural charm attracts others like moths to a flame, and they form relationships easily. In romantic relationships, they are loving but flighty, especially in the preliminary stages. It takes commitment and effort to keep them around, but it is well worth the work. They are passionate and dedicated when they eventually settle down.

Capricorn Totem Animal Is the Alligator

There is something primal about these magnificent beasts who have survived since prehistoric times, and their energy is found in Capricorns. Once they sink their teeth in, they never let go. Dogged determination and a strong jaw mean that nothing escapes their clutches. Capricorns are conventional beings and prefer order and rules rather than chaos.

Capricorns love to surround themselves with the best, but they are willing to work for their success. Sometimes they overthink things and become pessimistic, but that changes in a second when their enthusiasm takes over. As a partner, they are loyal, enthusiastic, and deeply loving.

Aquarius Totem Animal Is the Spider

These creative, hardworking, adaptable creatures represent the dark and light aspects of the Aquarian. They can be friendly or dangerous, and their appearance doesn't give you any clue about their nature. They are territorial and love to work alone, which makes them seem aloof but really, they are friendly when you get them in the right mood.

Their complex nature appeals to most partners, but they collaborate best with like-minded individuals. It takes time to get to know an Aquarian well, but they are with you for life once you do.

Pisces Totem Animal Is the Deer

Sensitive and shy deer can be spooked easily, yet they seem calm and peaceful when observed in their natural environment. They prefer a tranquil existence, and Pisces are just the same. They naturally shy away from conflict and vulgarity, preferring to mix with refined and cultured types. Their soft, gentle nature means they see the best in people but are hurt when their trust is broken.

Some of their negative traits include laziness and negativity, making them difficult partners. They tend to self-sabotage, so their partner needs to be extra aware of their moods and emotions.

Of course, totem animals have their personalities just like they do in real life. Some spirits are mischievous and playful, while others are more serious. Your totem animals will soon let you see their personalities.

Work with them and spend time communicating to fill your life with energy. Use an invoking phrase like "As I go about my day, my totem animal will find a way, come to me in love and peace and make my life be filled with dreams."

You can use a phrase of your own no matter how geeky you feel. If you have the confidence they are there, they will come. In Australia, Aboriginal people and Torres Strait Islanders often go on a "walkabout" to find their totem animal. Communing in nature will help you connect to them. Remember to set your intentions and have patience; they will appear when you're ready to receive them.

In nature, humans and animals have a symbiotic relationship with animals, where we all work together to make the world better. The spirit world is no different; totemic communications are simply a return to our original selves when the messages between the species were more prolific. Since the inception of the planet, man and animals were designed to work as a team; let's get back to that and embrace harmony and love.

Chapter 6: Sacred Geometry Symbols

Sacred geometry is the study of shapes and symbols and how they represent the spiritual meaning of life. It helps us understand the most common principle of life dating back to ancient Egyptian and Mesopotamian cultures, the intrinsic belief that nothing on Earth lives in isolation. The equation of life means that everything on Earth and in the heavens is connected, and the symbols in nature and geometry provide a detailed blueprint of connectivity.

Sacred geometry gives us a deep insight into our sense of natural alignment and allows us to use shapes and symbols to deepen our spiritual state. Practitioners use the focal points to induce meditative states by using shapes to form mandalas. These are formed by using geometric shapes to create a pleasing effect to decrease stress and help meditation.

The word mandala comes from the ancient language Sanskrit and means "circle" but has been adapted to describe all shapes. In nature, mandalas are all around us, flowers like daisies and roses or ripples on a water body. The first manmade examples originated in the first century B.C. made by monks in Buddhist temples, and the practice soon spread globally.

Although their origins were religious, today, mandalas are used by all cultures to represent the universe and mankind's search for self-awakening. The center represents the palace of our minds, and every layer brings an added element to the journey of life. One layer brings compassion; another represents wisdom and learning. There is no fixed number of layers, but each must be obtained before you can pass and grow closer to your final destination, the palace that represents your complete self-enlightenment.

Common Shapes and What They Mean

Triangle

In sacred geometry, the three-sided symbol represents the balance of the body, the mind, and the self. Its rising point symbolizes the connection to the heavens and gives a sense of raising consciousness. When the point is descending, it creates feminine energy associated with fertility and birth. When placed over the image of the female form, it points to the womb, symbolizing the root of all life.

Circle

The never-ending cycle of life, death, and rebirth: The circle has no beginning and no end, so it creates a symbol of unity between all forms of life and the spirit world. It represents the smallest atom to the largest planet and, as such, is indicative of all forms of cosmic existence. Some religions describe God as the geometer of the world because of the shape of the Earth.

Square

The epitome of solidity and foundation, the square is used to bring a stable base to sacred geometrical designs. Circles may represent the unity of life, but they work better when attached to a square.

Spiral

Found on seashells or used to represent the sun's orbit, the spiral is the symbol above and below. They are the most generic form of geometry found in nature and are also known as earth navels. Spirals were found at spiritual sites, including the Irish mound at Newgrange and the Portuguese prehistoric site of Piodao.

Sacred Geometry Symbols and What They Represent

Sometimes referred to as the language of the gods, these amazing symbols are some of the most mystical and magical representations of our abstract connection to the world and all who inhabit it.

The Flower of Life

This fascinating symbol originated in ancient times and is found in temples and religious buildings across the globe. It appeared on manuscripts and art in far-flung destinations and means different things to different cultures. The earliest depiction is thought to have been in ancient Egypt when archaeologists discovered the symbol drawn on granite at the Temple of Osiris.

It is mind-blowing that these intricate and beautiful drawings have survived for over 6,000 years. The images were created with an elevated level of precision and may have been an early representation of the Eye of the sun god Ra.

The symbol was only named the Flower of Life in the 1990s as the New Age movement embraced it and used it to represent more specific beliefs and sentiments. They use the classic seven circle flower shape to symbolize the shape of an embryo in its initial stages. A more elaborate thirteen circle flower is believed to be the basic design of the universe and the foundation for other sacred geometric designs.

Today the design can be found in various places. Worn as jewelry, like a tattoo, or as decorative pieces around the home, the flower of life is worn to show the intention of the wearer to attain spiritual enlightenment and find the true meaning of the universe. It is associated with the Kabbalah movement and is thought to have been the inspiration for their primary sacred geometrical symbol, the Tree of Life.

In Christianity, the seed of life, which is the seven circles version, is particularly relevant as it represents the seven days of the week and God's work to create the universe. It is mentioned as the Tree of Life in Genesis chapter 2, verse 9 in the Old Testament.

In Judaism, the Tree of life is made of ten sephiroth which represent various aspects of God. They are not meant to represent the higher being but are the medium that represents his qualities. The ten sephirot are divided into the three intellectual powers and the seven emotive powers, also referred to as the Three Mothers and the Seven Doubles.

The Sephirot Are Representations Of:

- Conceptual knowledge and wisdom
- Comprehension or the second stage of the intellectual process
- Knowledge following the maturity of the thought process
- Kindness or grace attained by the dispersion of the light and energy of the spirit
- Might or strength attained by exposure to the Divine light and revelation
- Beauty and mercy related to the emotional depth of the soul
- Conquest and victory related to the joy of emotional control
- The splendor of the Divine light
- Foundation of the basic level of attaining spiritual enlightenment
- Sovereignty is the ultimate sephirot relating to the ruling aspect of the Divine being

The Sri Yantra

This ritual sacred geometry diagram originates from Hinduism, the Vedic and Tantric cultures, and is one of the most powerful symbols in spiritual terms. Yantra means "to receive" or "to support" and is composed of three layers. There are two circles with lotus leaves containing a complex geometric figure surrounded by an outer perimeter which forms walls to contain the figure.

What Do the Features Mean?

The central form is overly complex and is made from nine triangles and a central dot. Five of the triangles point up, representing male energy, and the remaining four point downward, representing feminine energy. The central circular dot is the fundamental point of creation and signifies the origin of all living things.

The placement of the triangles is a geometrical wonder, and they merge to form forty-three smaller triangles that emphasize the importance of a crucial point. It focuses the mind on the conception of the universe and the cosmic force it took to complete.

The lotus flowers that form the circles indicate the importance of the fertile environment that surrounds us and the life force we all rely on. The circle shows the cyclical development of life and how we are all improving and developing.

The outer layer is composed of four t-shaped openings that are protective of their central components but can be accessed by those outside the world if they pass the initiation rites. The Yantra is a hallowed space, but it does show that the outside world can gain entrance if they are willing to put in the work.

Metatron's Cube

Named after the archangel, the geometric symbol is the equalizer of all the energy that enters the cosmic universe. It is made from platonic solids combined with thirteen circles that represent the archangels, with the circle of Metatron in the center.

What Are the Platonic Solids?

They are named after the philosopher Plato who highlighted the importance of their shapes when explaining the deeper truths about the universe. He connected the five shapes with the elements of the Earth and the Heavens.

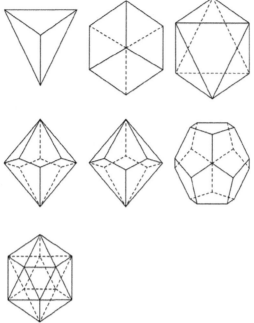

1. The Cube is representative of the Earth and is composed of six square faces, eight vertices, and twelve straight edges. Cubes are one of the most important geometric shapes, and all the faces are of equal dimension and are connected to the other four faces. It is also referred to as a regular hexahedron.

2. The tetrahedron is a triangular pyramid with four sides, six straight edges, and four apex corners. It is unusual among the platonic solids as it has no parallel faces, and all four corners are equidistant from each other.

3. Octahedron is a polyhedron with eight sides. It has twelve edges and six vertices. The most common version of the octahedron has eight equilateral triangles, with half of the total meeting at the summit. Four of the edges intersect, and it has six corner points.

4. The dodecahedron is a twelve-sided polyhedron with pentagonal sides. There are twenty corners, and three faces meet at each apex.

5. Icosahedron, as a general form, is a twenty-sided figure with equilateral triangular faces. It is the largest of the platonic solids and has a greater volume of area than any of the others.

These are the building blocks of Metatron's Cube and are symbolic of the journey of energy through the universe and how the cube maintains balance and equality. The spheres and straight edges emanate from the circular representation of Metatron and signify the unity of female and male energies.

As a point of energy, it is related to the butterfly effect that states if you tug at one string in the universe, the effect is felt throughout the stratosphere. Some beliefs feel that the central circle is the throne of God rather than Metatron and is the point through which all energy navigates.

The Eternal Knot

Also known as the endless knot, this ancient symbol was featured in Hindu, Buddhist, and Jainism to represent the Naga. These were members of a race of spirits that were semi-divine beings, half-human and half serpent. The protectors of Dharma and the protector of humans, they represented the ability to shed skins and be reborn into another form. They are both benevolent and malicious, and they indicate the two forms of human consciousness, the higher and lower forms of our true selves.

The symbol also represents the Buddhist concept of Samsara. The endless cycle of life and death and the karmic circle can only be completed when an individual attains spiritual enlightenment. In Celtic art, the knot is the mystic knot and represents the uninterrupted cycle of being. They began to appear in art from Ireland dating from the fifth century B.C.

The eternal knot is part of a series of symbols known as the Auspicious Symbols that have relevance to Buddhist beliefs. The other symbols are listed below.

- **Treasure Vase:** The meaning behind this symbol is the storage of material items to remove them from your desires. Placing your material possessions in the treasure vase means you can forget the negative emotions connected with material wealth and focus on your spiritual growth.
- **Dharma Wheel:** Composed of three main parts (the hub, the wheel, and the spokes), the Dharmas wheel represents Buddhist teachings and beliefs.
- **Victory Banner:** The symbol of achievement over obstacles and negativity. It is used to show how the Buddhist doctrine has triumphed over malevolent forces and emerged successfully.
- **Lotus Flower:** Usually pictured emerging from the mud of human detritus, it is a symbol of man's ability to rise above their base emotions and sufferings to become an enlightened part of the spiritual universe.
- **Golden Fish:** When pictured as a pair, they represent the mighty rivers Ganges and Yamuna and the fertility they bring to the areas on their banks. In more general terms, the symbol of the fish rising above the water symbolizes happiness and freedom.
- **Parasol:** The symbol of opulence and royalty in ancient times. Only the wealthy and important owned parasols, representing both physical and spiritual blessings. The parasol's shape signifies wisdom and empathy, both fundamental dogmas within Buddhism.
- **Conch:** This familiar shell-shaped symbol enhances vibrational energy and the joyful sounds of the Buddhist teachings.

Vesica Pisces

In Latin, the name Vesica Pisces translates to the bladder of a fish, but it represents a pair of symmetrically balanced circles in sacred geometry. Believed to be symbolic of the vagina of the Virgin Mary, most people associate it with Christian symbolism, but it has predated the Catholic church for thousands of years. Variations of the Vesica Pisces have been found in Norse traditions and Eastern mysticism. The symbol also had a prominent meaning in the ancient cultures of Greece, Egypt, India, and China and forms part of the more common Flower of Life.

When the circles cross, they form an oval shape named the mandala in the center, often used to frame a religious figure like Jesus or Mary. It has been called the fish of God and brings us back to that eternal joining of energy and creation. Without this bond, the rest of humanity and the universe would cease to exist. In Norse religions, the symbol is the merging of the God and Goddess, while Egyptian teachings tell us it is the cosmic womb of the Goddess Maat.

Whatever is the meaning behind the symbol, it is a powerful uniting energy and reminds us that all things come together and give each other life. The universe relies on that cohesion to continue evolving.

The Torus

This sacred core-level form in geometry is created with a swirling sequence of circles enclosed by a darker colored outer ring. Depending on your perspective, the energy depicts the descent from the spirit to matter or the rise to spirit from the matter. The circles create an ordered maelstrom of beginnings and journeys that take the eye forward before doubling back on itself, only to gain energy before commencing on its journey.

It reminds us that no matter how high we ascend, we must eventually return and touch base with our core. If an individual loses their connection with the torus, they spiral off into the ether because they become disassociated. The universe will eventually reconnect them, but it can be in this lifetime or in the next. This symbol reminds us that karmic energy decides our fate, and if we ignore universal dictates, it will let us go.

The Star of David

The star is mainly associated with the Jewish faith and has other esoteric meanings, especially in sacred geometry. It depicts the three sacred connections that form our very existence. The two triangles relate to the male and female energies, and seven separate building blocks emanate from the star's points. The six outer points are the emotional attributes of the divine being, while the center represents the foundation upon which the Divine is rooted.

How to Use Sacred Geometry

When you start to recognize the patterns and sequence in sacred geometry, your understanding of how we are connected to nature and the heavens will increase. Wear the symbol as jewelry or as a tattoo to show you're part of the process behind their energy. Maybe you aren't convinced they are as sacred as other people believe, and that's okay. Even if you just think they are works of art and will look good in your living room, use them like that; images of beauty make your home loom super modern and cool.

Whatever you get from these symbols is down to you and your perspective. If they make you feel connected to the universe, embrace that. If you just like their shape, embrace that. We are all individuals, and even the cosmic rulers know that free will is one of the key parts of human thinking, and they would never take that away.

Chapter 7: Runes and How to Use Them

The history of runes predates Christ by around two hundred years, but their precise origin is unknown. It is believed that the symbols evolved over time to serve as practical pieces used to communicate with the spirits and in other forms of divination. Different cultures attached various meanings to each symbol, and the runemasters of ancient times had their own interpretation.

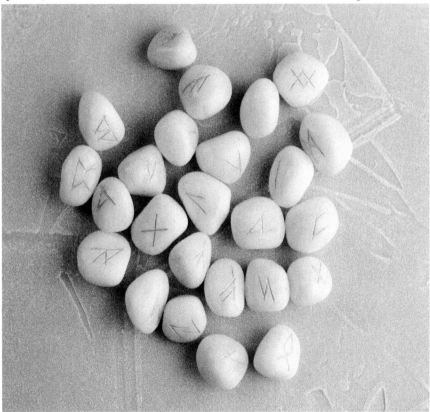

Each symbol represents a single letter in its purest forms, but they also contain a full word with a series of meanings. This sounds confusing, but it is how the runes are used. Runic grammar is a mixture of learned meanings and secret messages, which is why they are so powerful. Using runes to contact the ancient consciousness unleashes their potential for mystery and subliminal meanings.

The Elder Futhark runes are the most used today and are thought to have originated around 300 CE to 700 CE, the period just before the Viking age. They are the original runes and the easiest to understand. They were replaced by more intricate sets of runes as spoken communication forms evolved, but the Elder Futhark is the simplest way to convey a word or a message when it comes to divination. There are twenty-five runes in total, including the empty rune of Odin that has no symbol – but deep meaning.

Runes were undeniably influential in ancient times, and runemasters were revered seers called upon to connect with the divine and answer questions. They were used in rituals to bless their communities with happiness and love. They invoked the spirits to govern the weather for better crops, the seed for fertility and love, and used the figures to decorate their vessels and weapons.

Runemasters wore elaborate costumes that identified them as the experts. They were loved and adored, yet their powers also made them figures of fear. Unlike other levels of society, runemasters were often women as it was believed they had the power of second sight that made them better at interpreting the runes.

The Elder Futhark Runes and Their Meanings

MANNAZ, the Self

A letter M with the top pieces crossing forms an X between two straight lines. This rune is the symbol of self-effacement and reminds you to be humble. It is used to live a usual life in an unusual manner and be true to ourselves. Don't live an excessive life; balance the joy, and reflect upon your duties to live a reflective life that focuses on yourself.

GEBO, the Partnership or Gift

A simple X, this rune is pulled when a partnership is imminent. This can mean a relationship between partners or a business-style union. It tells you to be careful and make sure the connections you form are healthy with people who will respect your independence and the union.

FEHU, Property, Food, Animals

The letter F with a right slant and an extra branch on top is the symbol of fulfillment. This means different things to different people and could mean you will be given bounties from the Divine. This is a celebratory rune, but it also comes with caution, to be respectful of what you already have and not be distracted by ambition. Be vigilant and make sure you don't risk what you already have in the pursuit of reckless bliss.

OTHILA, Separation, and Withdrawal

This rune is a diamond with extended legs and indicates you need to shed your old persona and seek new experiences. It is the rune of moving on and leaving things behind. This can mean property, profit, or relationships. Have conviction and courage to go through with radical separation and emerge reborn. Don't worry about details; the universe will have your back.

URUZ, Sexual Power and a Wild Bull

This is a rune of endings and new beginnings. When drawn, it signifies the end of a chapter in your life and the need to move on. You may have to experience loss and grief, which are processes you must complete as you become the new enlightened self.

PERTH, Initiation, Concealment, and Secrets

This is the rune of soulful transformation. Other runes suggest that changes are based on the physical world, but this rune is a sign that you're changing spiritually from within. Nobody else will see these renewals of spirit, but you will feel them deeply. It's time to let go of negative energies and form new ways of evolving.

NAUTHIS, Compulsion and Necessity

A straight line with an offset bar, this rune is a sign that you're stagnating and need to make plans for the future. Are you stuck in a rut or feeling guilt or regret? It's time to forgive yourself and escape from the past. Restore balance by settling old scores and walking away harmoniously. Keep your emotions in check, and don't let anger hold you back.

INGWUZ, The God-Hero and Fertility

Two crosses are joined to make a central diamond; this rune is extremely powerful and influential. It signifies you need to fertilize your soil so you can grow. It's time for self-improvement and spiritual growth, so let go of your obstacles and discover new worlds. Choose your destination and prepare the ground for progress.

ALGIZ, Protection and Natural Barriers

This rune is a straight line with two upward arms like sticks and is the symbol of emotional control. It can be overwhelming when we transition, and this rune is a reminder to be strong. Your conduct is your strongest shield, and if you can control your responses during failure, you're a spiritual warrior. Even when you don't win, you learn from the experiences.

EIHWAZ, The Yew Tree and Defensive Forces

This tilted reversed Z figure is the rune of defense and advises us to be patient. Frustration never helps a situation, so the universe will comply if you can master your emotions and wait for positivity to be part of your life. As you contemplate your destiny, learn to acknowledge behaviors that are holding you back and abandon them. Do the right thing, and you will avoid difficulties.

ANSUZ, The Messenger Rune and Signals

In Norse terms, this rune was representative of Loki, the messenger of Odin. It is pulled to encourage you to look for signals and signs from the universe and show you how to progress. Be more attentive when you meet people and view accidental encounters as meaningful. Always recognize the opportunity to learn from your peers and the chance to teach the less fortunate people you encounter.

WUNJO, Joy and Light

The symbol looks like a P with a pointed upper stem. It is the rune that signals you have arrived at a harmonious place. The rune is the fruit-bearing branch and bestows its blessing on you both emotionally and physically. It shows a balanced view of your place in the world, and you can manage the relationship between your ego and the higher self. It signifies you're on the right track and living a positive and honest existence. Continue like this, and you will reach fulfillment and enlightenment.

JERA, Harvest, Full Cycle, and Fertility

Two arrowheads pointing left and right signal success; they indicate a fulfilling sense of achievement and praise for your devotions. It is a reminder that success and enlightenment don't come with quick results. A cycle of time must pass before you can harvest your successes. We see the perfect example of the yearly cycle of growth and liberation in nature.

KENA, Opening, Torch

The left-pointing arrowhead is the rune of awakening, a bright, fresh start, and the extradition of the darkness. It is a rune of activity connected to the morning. When the darkness has lifted, you will see clearly what is relevant in your life and what has been hampering you. The morning association could mean you need to concentrate on your job or improve your clarity and focus on your family. Whatever the morning means for you, this rune tells you to prioritize it.

TYR, The God Tiu and Warrior Energy

This upward-facing arrow is the ultimate rune for courage and strength. Tiu is the Germanic and English god of the sky and war known for his sense of justice. The day Tuesday is named after him, and he is influential in the formalities of battles. He is an enigmatic figure who teaches perseverance and trust in the will of the Divine. The rune makes you question your priorities and examine how you use your energy. It shows you the path to your inner foundation and how it affects your life. Find strength in the warrior god's power and learn from his patience and dedication.

BERKANA, Growth and Rebirth

The letter B with pointed arms is the rune of growth. It symbolizes the time to move on and complete another cycle of your existence. It teaches us to connect to nature and be influenced by its flow. Scatter your resistances and take the path that flows between them to achieve your goals with the least obstacles. This rune is a warning that there may be characters or events in your future deliberately trying to hold you back. Be patient and understand that they aren't insurmountable and are merely distractions from the growth of your new life.

EHWAZ, Movement and Advancement

This classic shape of the letter M signifies gradual progress and steady energy fueling your change and rebirth. It reminds us that even when we miss the chance to do something, we will be given the opportunity further down the line. Stop worrying that other people seem to be progressing at a faster rate than you. When you feel the time is right, take the next step and keep control of your life and your journey. Some opportunities aren't for you; just because you have them doesn't mean you should take them.

LAGUZ, Driving Force, Flowing Water

A straight line with a downward right pointing arm, this rune is a cautionary sign to make sure you aren't overestimating your life force or working towards material objects while neglecting the natural flow of your energy. It reminds us that natural forces dictate all things, and when we try to accelerate them, we interrupt the universe's balance. Ambition is good, providing it doesn't become excessive and is in tune with the intuitive knowledge that guides you.

HAGALAZ, Natures Destructive Elements

The shape of this rune is an H with a slanted central bar, and it represents the need to identify the damaged areas of your life, repair them, and find change and freedom. Rise above the confines of material needs and discover your spiritual self. Your psyche needs to experience the freedom your physical self takes for granted and soar into the ether. It may experience some elemental damage, but it will only grow stronger and experience resolution.

THURISAZ, Gateway, the Destination for Contemplation

A straight line with a right-pointing arrowhead, this rune tells you to stop for a while and reconsider where your life is going. Gateways normally represent a passing area or the symbolic change of environments, but this gateway is different. It is the area of non-doing and maybe a symbol that your mental process isn't as strong as it can be. This is the spiritual version of stopping and smelling the coffee.

DAGAZ, Change and Transformation

This butterfly-shaped rune is a signal of success and progress. You have reached a point when your transformation is changing your life forever. The energy behind this rune is thrusting and energetic. It gives you the confidence to leap into the next phase of your spiritual awakening even when you feel unsure of what lies beyond.

ISA, Torpidity and Hindrance

This stark straight line is a sure sign the winter of your spiritual awakening is upon you. There is a stagnant feel to your life, and you may feel trapped and alone. Take solace from the fact that all-natural cycles have periods of stagnation. Think of the bleak cold months when nothing grows but remember that it is also a period to recharge and regroup. Find out why you're stuck and what you can do about it. Sometimes you can't control circumstances, so take a back seat and wait for them to pass or resolve themselves. Yielding to them should be seen as a badge of honor and courage.

RAIDHO, Communication and Reconciliation

The figure R is a strong sign you need to regroup. Your alignment may be slightly out of line, and your energies are clashing. You have an intrinsic value that is being compromised by your lack of communication. Are there some outside influences that are distracting you from your journey? Do you have the positive influences you need to progress? At times, our strength is enough to fuel us, but sometimes we need to lean on others. Make sure they give you the right support and don't interfere in your spiritual progress.

SOWILU, The Energy of the Sun and Completeness

This lightning bolt symbol is a power rune that gives you a sense of wholeness. It doesn't mean you completed your journey, there is no rune for that, but it is a sign that the life force is there for you. Use it to recharge and regroup, perhaps meditate on the surge of power at your fingertips.

ODIN, the God Odin and the Sense of Mystery

This is an empty rune with no symbol or markings. If you draw this rune, it means you must surrender your control of fate and let the universe guide you. It isn't a negative rune; it is a signal from the Divine that they have you, and your journey isn't a lone mission.

How to Cast Runes

There are many ways to cast your runes. The method below will help you become comfortable with this form of divination. The meanings attached to the stones are merely a foundation for you to work with, and their interpretations are a guide. As with other divination methods, the most important thing to remember is what the runes say to you. They are a means to communicate with your subconscious and find out what will happen if you take a certain path.

They are not fortune-telling instruments. Just like scrying, they reflect what you feel will happen even though your conscious mind isn't aware of the concept. They won't tell you if and when you will get married or how many kids you will have; they only give insights into how circumstances will change if you do.

Casting Runes

This is the term used for tossing the runes and should be done in an ordered fashion. Cast the runes from east to west on a white cloth. The runes should be taken from a leather pouch where they are kept when not in use.

- **Daily Reading**

Sit in a quiet place and form a question in your mind. Take a single stone from the pouch and focus on what it means. Feel the surface and hold it tight until you feel the message reaching your mind.

- **The Three-Stone Spread**

Choose three separate stones and cast them on the cloth. Make a note of their position as well as their meanings. The first stone is representative of the physical self, the second is the mental state, and the third relates to your spirituality. If your question is time-related, the stones may represent the past, the present, and the future. How you interpret them is intensely personal and open to influences.

- **The Five Stone Cross**

Choose five stones to work with. Lay one of them at the center and place the remaining four at the cardinal points. The central stone deals with your current dilemmas or mental state. The northern stone is your preferred outcome after you have dealt with the other issues. The southern stone is something that is inevitable and needs to be accepted. The western stone is an obstacle that must be faced, and the eastern stone represents something from the past that needs to be left behind.

- **The Grid**

Take all the stones out of the pouch and lay them in a grid formation. Close your eyes and run your non-dominant hand slightly above them until you feel an energy that makes your hand tingle. That is the stone that holds your answer.

- **The Full Cast**

Cast all the stones across your white cloth and let them fall randomly. Pose your question as they fall, and the stones (or stone) that attracts you will contain your answer.

Caring for Your Runes

Your white cloth should protect your sacred stones, but you should replace them if they get damaged or dirty. Always keep them safe in their pouch and never let other people use them. They are charged with your energy, and any cross-contamination will affect the readings.

Chapter 8: Symbols of Protection

When you do activities in your daily lives, you take protection seriously. Maintaining and keeping your car and home safe and taking out insurance to make sure you're covered in the worst-case scenario. When you do something dangerous, you use protective clothing and equipment to keep yourself safe, and when you go to a social space, you expect it to be protected.

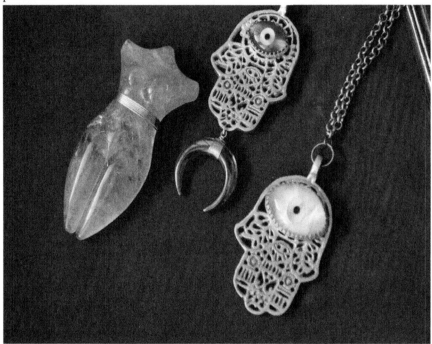

The same principles apply to your spiritual self. Why would you take such care to protect your physical form and neglect protecting your spiritual and emotional self? Different regions and cultures offer a range of symbols that can be utilized to keep you safe and protected in regular life and when you're performing rituals or spells.

Some of these symbols have already been mentioned, but it is worth re-examining them in their specific role as defense mechanisms that will shield you from negativity and evil. The spiritual world can be scary, and sometimes you must deal with negative energies and entities; these symbols will help you stay secure and repel their energies.

The Hamsa

A decorative hand-shaped symbol that contains the eye of protection, this Middle Eastern symbol is found in the teachings of many diverse cultures. The protection element of the eye defines it as one of the most powerful shields available.

The Triquetra

The number three features in many powerful unions. In Christianity, it represents the Holy Trinity of the Father, the Son, and the Holy Ghost. In cosmology, it represents the three domains, earth, sea, and sky, while in philosophy, it is representative of the three aspects of humankind, the physical, mental, and spiritual states. The triquetra is a three-pointed symbol with interwoven circles and curves with no definite beginning or end, suggesting an eternal cloak of the sanctuary.

The Cacti

This three-armed version of the hardy plant is symbolic of the cacti's strength and endurance. They thrive in the most desolate areas and are an emblematic way to protect yourself and your home with endless care and attention. In some cultures, it represents maternal love, one of the strongest forms of protection known to man.

The Turtle

This symbolizes the turtle's strength representing long life and the strength of its hard shell. Native Americans identified the turtle as the symbol of longevity and sanctuary.

The Scarab

This decorative beetle is often associated with Ancient Egypt. The body of the image symbolizes protection against the dark forces, and the wings show the essence of rebirth. The symbol has become an international ideogram of security and strength.

Egyptian Knife

Highly decorated with a deadly curved blade, this knife was often depicted with deities tasked with protecting the Pharos. It has images of the sun and moon to imbue the duality of solar and lunar energy. It is believed the blade could slay malevolent creatures with just one sharp cut.

Thor's Hammer

Thor was the ultimate warrior in Norse and Asantric religions and teachings and could slay the strongest foes with his mighty hammer. This symbol is a decorated image that brings power to those who use it. The intricate carvings show that even the deadliest weapons can be aesthetically pleasing.

The Helm of Awe

The thick black circle containing a central disc with eight elaborate tridents protruding from the middle symbolizes terror. The Viking warriors often tattooed this image on their foreheads before going into battle to ensure victory and strike terror into their enemies. The inclusiveness of the image is meant to encourage unity and prevent rebellions within the ranks.

Nazar Boncugu

The black dot surrounded by a pale blue circle, a narrow white circle, and then encompassed by a dark blue border is another version of the protective eye. It dispels bad energy and promotes positivity and love.

Bagua Mirror

A spiderweb design surrounds a hollow circle with a series of dots on the perimeter. Feng shui experts use this symbol. It can often be found on the exterior of buildings facing out to deflect bad energy away from the structure. It is especially effective when used to protect corners.

The Arrow

Symbolically, arrows depict motion and progress, but they are also effective protective images.

The Solar Cross

This symbol was first found in the Bronze Age and characterized wealth and power. In Celtic circles, kings and queens wore it to signal their regality, but the meaning has changed in modern times. The solar cross is often found in places that promote a safe haven for travelers and those in need of shelter.

The Eye of Horus

The eye of protection is contained in a triangle circled by a checkered ring. Egyptians used this symbol to protect both the living and the dead from evil. It was included in the ceremonies to send people on their last journey to the underworld to ensure they got there safely. It is more associated with health matters and protection from ill-health in modern times.

Gila Monster

In nature, the Gila monster is a venomous lizard that can grow as long as sixty centimeters and is considered the master of survival. In spiritual terms, it is a symbol comprised of a diamond body with four separate horned legs and a head containing one eye. It is a positive active symbol that promotes the energy to take action and be purposeful.

Thunderbirds

Often seen in Native American art and rituals, thunderbirds have an eagle's head topping two wings perched on three horns. The horns are emblematic of spiritual energy, while the body of the thunderbird gives strength and power to the wearer.

The Dragonfly

The dragonfly lives between the air and the water in nature, and this elaborately decorative symbol unites the two energies. This unity helps you experience physical and spiritual activities and blend the two to realize self-transformation.

The Tree of Life

This sacred symbol is a reminder that we are all part of the universe, and when we face difficulties, we can call on that strength and unity. In some cultures, it is the ultimate symbol of humanity, and in Islamic culture, it is the sign of immortality.

Ankh

This symbol has the male strength of the cross and feminine loop combined. It was seen as the key to life in Ancient Egyptian teachings. It protects the wearer by guarding their life force and linking it to the nurturing air and water sources.

Yin and Yang

The black and white circle symbolizes unity and was used to protect couples in Chinese philosophy. This could mean the traditional form of a couple, the man and woman, but it also includes less conventional pairings. The corresponding dots in the solid shapes show that we need others in our lives, and their seeds are found nestling in our psyche.

Caduceus

Originally the staff carried by the winged God Hermes, this decorative symbol is now associated with medicinal institutions and organizations and is globally displayed by doctors and hospitals. The short staff comprises two intertwined serpents topped by a magnificent pair of outstretched wings. In Greek mythology, it represented immortality and enlightenment.

Wish-Bone

Most people know the wishbone ritual when you have a chicken dinner. Two people loop their pinkie fingers around the two bones and pull. The winner will be blessed with good luck for the rest of the day. The symbol representing the wishbone is used as a lucky charm and signifies a new beginning and the chance to safely move on from the past with a clean sheet.

Crossed Spears

Also known as the crossed arrows or the crossroads, this is a universal symbol for protection against evil. Pagans use the symbol to celebrate the Sabbat Litha and the dawn of the year's longest day. Other cultures use it as a barrier to prevent bad energy and evil from crossing the borders of their homes. The spears are especially significant to warriors and symbolize the strength of their fighting spirit and their will to win. The spears also appear in the witches' runes and are a powerful metaphor for change and rebirth.

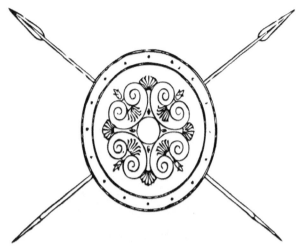

The Hexagram

Worn as a signet ring by King Solomon, the hexagram is a significant part of Jewish culture. Its six points attract the attention of six individual gods, protecting the wearer from the evil that may come from any direction. Its shape is found in nature and relates to the heart of our origins. Use this powerful symbol to awaken your subconscious and find the hidden wisdom we are all born with. This wisdom will protect you from ignorance and harm. Upgrade your programs with the hexagon, and you will immediately feel the benefits.

Bind Rune

Talismans and decorative pieces will often combine runes to incorporate two or more runes to strengthen their intent. The symbol you create will be tailored to your needs and imbued with your intent. We will explore bind runes in a later chapter.

The Sign of Mars

A circle with an arrow protruding to the top right corner is a symbol of protection during troubling times. It gives you the strength and bravery to stand up to those who would do you harm and confront them. It can be used to attract positive energy and repel negative forces, so you need to be focused when you use this image. Mars is the keeper of our darkest secrets and can be trusted to be your fellow combatant when you need him.

Inanna's Knot

This is a stylized bundle of reeds that resembles a staff carried by Catholic bishops. It symbolizes fertility and growth and is symbolic of the reed-built boat the Goddess Inanna built for the world when the malevolent force Enoki flooded the world to wipe out humankind.

Celtic Shield Knot

This four-part symbol comprises a circular shape that was used to protect the wounded on battlegrounds from death or further attack. Warriors would often decorate their shields with this symbol to invoke the protective energy of God.

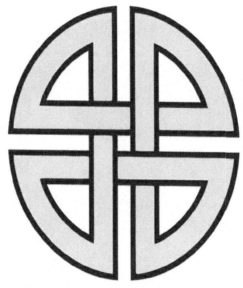

Tyet

Another ancient Egyptian symbol is an extension of the *ankh* symbol. The standard shape has been decorated with downward turned arms and has the emblematic motif that relates to the beliefs of the group of people displaying it. Depending on the God or Goddess it represents, these can be bovine or bats. Amulets with the Tyet engraved on them were often buried with the dead to keep them safe on their journey to the underworld.

The Laurel Wreath

The circle of laurel leaves will often appear with the image of a roman warrior's head in silhouette in the center. It is a symbolic image of victory and was worn on Roman emperors' heads as a sign of their imperial power and authority. In the ancient Pythian Games held in honor of Apollo, the winners of the athletic festivals were adorned with laurel wreaths to signify their victory. It has been associated with the significance of the medals at the Olympic medals. Its protective qualities originate in the belief that lightning never strikes a laurel tree, so its leaves are the perfect foil for evil forces in both beast and human form.

Akoko Nan

An African symbol that represents the leg of a chicken or hen because of a popular African proverb, "The leg of hen steps on the child chick but it doesn't kill the chick," which indicates the strength and protection parents have for their children.

Drangue

Albanian in origin, this jagged bolt of lightning represents the heavy thunderstorms that are found in the area. The Drangue is a semi-human being born with a caul and four wings that gave it the strength to battle the forces of nature. The Drangue is mankind's protector and fights the Kulshedra, who sends lightning bolts and other natural disasters to devastate humankind.

The Labyrinth

This maze-like symbol was used to confuse and trap evil spirits within its complicated design in Greek culture. It also represents the circle of life and the long journey to the Divine. Its hypnotic image focuses on your mind, and when you begin to meditate, you can follow the lines to create a peaceful mental state.

The Shaligram

The original Shaligram stone was believed to have been found on the banks of the Gandaki river in Nepal. The stone contained a natural design that looked like a fossil or a decorative conch shell. It is associated with the god Vishnu, a powerful protective force in Hindu teachings. It is used to repel negative energy and harmful forces.

The Cornucopia

Also known as the horn of plenty, it is a symbol of a conical vessel overflowing with fruits, bread, flowers, and nuts. It traditionally signifies abundance but is used as protection against poverty and hunger. It was used by the Roman God Bona Dea, who was responsible for the protection of Rome.

The Bow and Arrow

Often associated with Cupid, this symbol is more romantic than most. Its powerful union between the female energy of the bow and the male energy of the arrow brings strength and power to the wearer and forms a powerful symbol of energy.

Om

Also spelled as Aum or Ohm, this symbol originated from Buddhism but is seen at all levels of society. The bottom curve represents the waking state; the middle curve is the dream state, while the upper curve is the deeper state of unconsciousness. A crescent tops these curves and represents the Maya, the state of mind that allows you to connect with the divine. It represents the infinite language and knowledge that protect humanity from themselves and the negative beings that would stand in the way of their spiritual enlightenment.

Algiz

A Norse representation of an elk surrounded by a protective circle is a powerful symbol that inspires divine protection. It increases your luck and brings prosperity and abundance.

Hecate's Wheel

A maze-like series of curves surrounding a six-sided star, this symbol is the sign of Hecate, the Greek goddess of the sea, the sky, and earth. She was especially concerned with keeping families safe. The spiral star at the center represents rebirth and the beginning of a new journey.

Horseshoe

This familiar symbol was first seen in Roman culture as a recognizable sign of good luck. In the Middle Ages, it was believed that evil spirits were kept away by horseshoes because of their fire-resistant qualities. They were hung in doorways to keep homes safe and protected and were often found on bedroom walls to ward off nightmares. Some people believe that hanging a horseshoe with the opening pointing down leads to a period of bad luck.

Chi Rho

One of the earliest forms of Christogram, this symbol comprises a combination of Greek letters chi and rho of the alphabet. A monogram emerges that looks like the marriage of the English letters X and P. The word Chi Rho is pronounced *keeroe* and means *Christ*. This symbol invokes the power of the heavens to watch over you and keep you free from harm.

How to Use Protection Symbols

The nature of symbolism means that it can be used in everyday life. Use them to create designs for tattoos or jewelry, or get them printed on your clothing. There are hundreds of unique ways to use these symbols and keep yourself and your home safe. Create artwork to hang on your walls or decorate your home and make a statement to the universe that you're receptive and ready to embrace symbolism.

T-shirts and other apparel are available from online stores like Amazon or more specialized stores like Redbubble and Tee Public. Jewelry based on spiritual symbols is extremely popular today and can be worn every day or customized for special occasions like weddings and communions. Give symbolic jewelry as a gift to keep your friends safe and introduce them to a more spiritual life.

Protection symbols are iconic and will bring beauty and safety wherever you place them. Doorways and windows are classic portals for negative energy, so hanging a talisman or pendant will seal your home and defend it against negativity. They are also perfect to use as a point of focus when meditating.

Chapter 9: Other Magical Symbols and What They Mean

We have already acknowledged the importance of symbols and how they represent the deep meanings implanted in our subconscious. We are hardwired to react to certain images and be influenced by them. Just like the pen is mightier than the sword, the world of symbolism is a constant reservoir of experience and the collective unconscious.

Knowing what these symbols mean and how they affect you can give a deeper insight into the blueprint of your soul, your raison détre, and connects you to the universe. This section will look at the hidden meanings behind some of the most universal symbols and discover some images from other cultures that may influence your life.

Aboriginal Symbols

Aborigines are the indigenous race of people who live in Australia and can trace their history back to the beginning of time. Originally, they had no written language as such, and they relied on symbols and artwork to communicate. They used a series of dots and lines to create complex and simple artwork to pass on their knowledge and experiences to the generations.

Today they are more integrated with modern society, but their heritage is a huge part of their identity. Studying their symbols gives us an insight into communication in its basest form, which conveys multiple meanings to different people.

- **The Budgerigar**

This symbol is a central dot surrounded by two rings with a trail of T symbols forming a path and tells the story of the budgerigar and its part in Aboriginal hunting methods. The circles represent the tree chosen as a home by the bird, and the trail of claw prints shows how they circle and find food. Early hunters followed the trail to find edible foods and fertile grounds with water sources.

- **Campsite**

This classic Aboriginal icon depicts several concentric circles with marks representing the people who live there and their homes. Two solid windbreaks mark the outer barriers of the camp and the security they provide. Each symbol is meaningful and signifies something.

Ancient Persian Symbols

Ancient Persia was a mystical place and one of the first established civilizations ever recorded. It was influenced by numerous cultures and was successfully invaded by some of the most powerful dynasties of the ancient world. Each conquest meant that Persian symbolism became influential throughout history, and some became popular in modern art.

- **Simurg**

An ancient Persian immortal bird who guarded the land and acted as a messenger between the Gods and humans, this scaled bird has a dog's head, lions' claws, and an elaborate tail of a peacock. It often has a human face with kind and benevolent features.

- **The Griffin**

This popular mythical creature can often be found in modern fiction, movies, and television. The body of a lion is topped with the head and wings of an eagle; griffins are the guardians who watch over our most prized possessions.

Chinese Symbols

Symbols from Asia have become popular in modern symbolism because they are aesthetically pleasing and convey messages of joy and love. They are easy to replicate and bring happiness and love to all.

- **Fu**

Meaning blessing, good luck, or fortune, this is one of the most popular characters used by the Chinese. It is especially relevant during the Chinese New Year and can be found hanging in the doorways of houses and apartments.

- **Lu**

In the past, this symbol represented a man's salary, but it has evolved to symbolize more than just financial luck. It represents health, wealth, and overall happiness and is worn as jewelry or sported as a tattoo.

- **Xi**

Happiness and joy. Xi is a symbol of both and brings good luck to newlyweds. It is posted everywhere at Chinese weddings.

- **He**

Harmony is an integral part of Chinese culture, and this symbol will bring you harmonious relationships with others.

- **De**

The symbol of virtue and morality, it brings kindness to the heart and soul and promotes a virtuous life.

Dream Symbols

When we sleep, we dream. Sometimes we remember what these dreams are, and it is obvious what has fueled them, but sometimes the most random images appear and can leave us bewildered. It doesn't matter if you believe these images are sent by the spiritual world, archangels, and angels, or they originated in your subconscious; they are sent for a reason. Symbolism is a way to understand your life and how it is responding to certain situations. Understanding the symbolic meanings will help you decipher the messages you're being sent.

- **Water**

Dreaming of rivers or waterfalls is common because it represents your emotions. If the water source is dangerous or you feel threatened, it can mean you're feeling unsettled and worried in real life. If you dream about waves or waterfalls, you're feeling overwhelmed, while calm bodies of water mean you're at peace.

- **Baby**

In normal life, having a baby is a joyous occasion and is considered a blessing of nature. In dream form, it can mean an intention to become a parent, but it can also mean a vulnerability and a wish to escape the responsibilities of adult life.

- **Snake**

Commonly seen as a symbol of traitors, the snake also represents mystical forces within us. When you dream of a snake, it means you're ready to enhance your life with primal energy and become more enlightened. When a snake fails in your dreams, it means you're struggling for fortune.

- **Clocks**

Any form of timepiece shows you have feelings that time is getting away from you. If you dream of winding a clock, it signifies the start of a new period where you can change direction and find success. If the alarm goes off, it means you need to make a decision.

- **Tunnels**

Dreaming about tunnels means you're ignoring certain parts of your mind. Explore the deepest corners of your psyche and find those hidden thoughts. Tunnels also represent birth and death, which can be a physical or metaphorical events.

Flower Symbols

Throughout history, flowers have been used to symbolize love, war, and allegiance. The War of the Roses was so-called because the two opposing sides wore white and red roses on their shields. Traditionally roses are the flower of love, but other blooms have significant meanings, which are explained below.

- **Iris**

In ancient Greece, mourners would plant these flowers on their loved one's graves in the hope they would attract the Goddess Oris to lead them to the underworld. French kings also wore the iris on their shields, and the symbol evolved to become the fleur-de-lis, the ultimate French symbol of power and royalty. Iris flowers are a symbol of hope and love.

- **Pansy**

In the 19th century, English suitors sent pansies to the object of their desire to indicate they were feeling amorous. They were also sent to indicate when you're missing someone and wish they would return. Today it is the symbol of love, kindness, and free-thinking.

- **Poppy**

Ancient Greeks and Romans used the poppy to signify health, fertility, and passion. The farmers would plant poppies in cornfields to encourage the crops to grow and promote prosperity. Poppies are used to remember the following dead warfare and are worn to remember the soldiers who have fallen.

- Cyclamen

The symbol of the Virgin Mary; the shape of the petals seems to represent a head lowered in prayer, while the red color is indicative of Mary's heart bleeding about the death of her son. In Japanese culture, the cyclamen is the flower of love and tenderness.

- **Anemone**

Western cultures use the anemone to represent good luck, but it is a symbol of bad fortune in the East. In Greek mythology, Aphrodite wept tears that formed anemones when she mourned the death of Adonis. Anemones are often used to ward off bad health and promote healing.

Graveyard Symbols

We all know that death is the one thing that unites us, but different cultures deal with it in different ways. Graveyards and cemeteries are the places where the bodies lie while their souls travel to the next plane. This makes them a place for celebration in some cultures, while others treat them with somber respect. The symbols displayed in cemeteries give us an insight into the beliefs and traditions the family of the departed subscribe to.

- **Flaming Torch**

A blazing crossed pair of torches traditionally meant death, but it is a symbol of divine power in Christian graveyards. In ancient times a single flame represented mourning and the pain of loss.

- **Cherubs**

Because of their childlike features, cherubs are often used to adorn children's graves. They symbolize the angelic forces that guard the soul on the way to heaven.

- **Hourglass**

A common sight on graves from the past. They are used to encourage those left behind to embrace life. An hourglass with wings shows the fleeting passage of time and represents our brief time on Earth.

- **Urn**

In Ancient Egypt, the internal organs of the dead were kept in urns, and today we keep the ashes of passed loved ones in decorated urns. Thus, urns are often depicted in graveyards. Draped examples signify the connection between the living and the dead.

- **Tree**

Tree symbolism is universally representative of the bridge between the heavens and the earth. In Africa, the baobab tree is sacred, and communities bury their wise men under the baobab to stay connected to them and benefit from their knowledge even after death.

Irish Symbols

The Celts have a rich history filled with old traditions and symbols. Their character and love of life are represented by some of the most common symbols we see daily. These images have become part of our culture; from the legends, myths, and folklore, they form strong associations with love and happiness.

- **The Claddagh**

The two hands holding a heart wearing a crown is perhaps the epitome of romance. The trinity symbolizes the perfect union between male and female energies, with the central heart on display to show their love to the world.

- **The Shamrock**

The three-leafed plant automatically makes you think of Ireland and all things Irish. It is believed that St. Patrick used symbolism to promote Christianity, using the three leaves to represent the holy trinity. The shamrock is the symbol of good luck and prosperity.

- **The Irish Harp**

The trademark of Guinness, the harp, is symbolic of the famous Irish hospitality. Entertaining their guests and bringing music to life is the Irish way, and the harp symbolizes their ethos. It has been displayed on flags and banners for centuries and featured prominently in the Irish Rebellion campaign.

- **Rainbows**

A colorful reminder that folklore tells the tale of the leprechaun and his pot of gold hidden at the end. In symbolism, the rainbow represents an idea or goal that is unlikely to be achieved. Finding that pot of gold could mean your wildest dreams will come true.

Love Symbols

When you're in love, words can seem redundant. You want to show your love uniquely and powerfully, so you use symbols to express and show your partner the depth of your feelings. Love symbols are fun and can attract passion into your life, even if you're single. Use these symbols to show you're ready and willing to find love.

- **The Heart**

Possibly the most recognizable symbol ever, the heart represents our core, the emotional and moral depth of our being. When we wear our heart on our sleeve, we show vulnerability and strength of character.

- **Ribbons and Frills**

In days gone by, a lady would bestow her favorite knight with a scarf or ribbon to show her allegiance before they jousted. In more recent times, ladies would drop their handkerchiefs to see if a gentleman would pick them up and signal their romantic intentions. Of course, today's females are stronger and would be mortified if they had to resort to such tactics. However, they can still show interest by wearing extra feminine apparel when they are with their partners. Displaying that extra layer of femininity can get the pulses racing.

- **Cupid**

Cupid is known as the God of desire, shown with a bow and arrow, who reportedly shoots the bow into the heart of your chosen mate. Although the image is quite kitsch today, it still appears on Valentine's Day cards and gifts for those who love romantic icons.

Motherhood Symbols

There have always been mothers, and whichever culture you study, they are held in regard and worshipped as the bringers of life. Symbols representing this fact have been around for as long as the birth process. Their roots are at the beginning of intelligent forms of communication. Among these symbols are some of the most enduring symbols that have survived changes in society and culture.

- **The Circle**

A simple circle is perhaps the most compelling symbol of motherhood, the endless cycle of birth and death. Native Americans added a dot to the center to symbolize "woman" and the circle to convey the concept of birth.

- **The Crow Mother**

The Crow Mother was the Hopi religion's ultimate nurturing and loving mother. She brought abundance to the people in the form of a basket of sprouts, and her love for her children was unrivaled. She brought yucca leaves to rituals and taught her people how to use them as weapons.

- **Flowering Cactus**

In Native America, the yellow flower produced by a cactus was thought to be the ultimate symbol of birth in the most inhospitable environments. It symbolizes the strength and endurance all mothers must have to raise their children in even the most difficult circumstances.

Political Symbols

Politics rules the world, and the parties that seek to become rulers need to show their potential voters what they represent. We are beginning to understand that just one image can be more powerful than a thousand words, so it makes sense that political parties are easily recognizable by their symbols.

- **The Donkey**

In 1828, Andrew Jackson was dubbed the "jackass" of the Democratic Party by his rivals. Instead of taking offense, he embraced the image and turned it positive. He used the symbol of a donkey on his campaign posters and was duly elected as President. While he was in office, he commissioned a popular cartoonist of the time to embellish the image with red, white, and blue stripes incorporating white stars. It is still used as the symbol of the Democratic Party and shows stubbornness and humility.

- **The Elephant**

Around the same period, the Civil War was raging, and the Republican party used the phrase "seeing the elephant" to describe experience gained even during loss. The same cartoonist who embellished the donkey for the Democrats created the image of the elephant for the Republicans. It stands for strength and stability and is used in India to represent royalty. Some cultures believe the elephant carried the world on its back.

- **The Hammer and Sickle**

Communism is rooted in creating a fairer place for the working classes, so the use of implements that represent the working class and peasants made the parties' ideals apparent immediately. Together they form a symbol of strength against repression by the ruling classes.

Religious Symbols

Perhaps the category where symbolism is most significant. Religions and their followers are deeply connected to the artwork, symbols, and rituals that foster solidarity and make them easily recognizable to other members or potential followers. They are designed to represent the moral values that show the ethos of the organization they front.

- **The Happy Human**

Humanism is a philosophical stance that focuses on the individual state of every human and the potential for social interaction and creating a society that embodies the Latin concept of *humanitas*. Although it is seen as a modern concept, humanism first emerged in pre-Socrates Greek teachings. Philosophers attempted to explain the correlation between human law and nature.

The happy human symbol is a design created in 1965. It represents a human form raising its hands in the air as if it is cheering. Humanist organizations are established across the world to give non-religious people the chance to work together to form a fairer society and a secular state. They perform regular rituals like weddings and funerals without emphasizing religious themes.

- **The Ouroboros**

This powerful symbol depicts a snake or a dragon swallowing its tail to represent the circle of infinity. It was adopted by Gnosticism and

Hermeticism, who used the symbol to enforce the belief that a remote divine being created the world. They teach the belief that esoteric knowledge, the gnosis, is the key to the redemption of the human spirit. Self-reflection and constantly recreating ourselves is the key to the survival of humanity.

- **Buddha Eyes**

Virtually every Buddhist shrine in Nepal has this symbol featured on the four sides of the main tower. They are highly decorated eyes with elaborate eyebrows on either side of a noose fashioned from a question mark. The symbol represents the all-seeing eyes of Buddha and his wisdom. It is a way to represent the most important tenets of Buddhism, nirvana, enlightenment, and omniscience.

- **Hands of God**

The four rake-like parts of this symbol represent the hands that intervene in the affairs on Earth by the Almighty. They aren't a specific religious symbol but are generically used by religious groups. During the Medieval Ages, the depiction of Jehovah as a fully formed human was considered disrespectable, so artists were encouraged to use just the hand and sometimes part of the arm. A popular depiction of the hand of God appears in Michelangelo's *Creation of Adam*, where a perfect human hand connects with Adam's hand and forms an electrical connection.

- **Angel Moroni**

The unofficial symbol of the Church of Jesus Christ Latter-Day Saints, Moroni, is the angel that reportedly visited the founder of the religion, Joseph Smith, in 1823. He is depicted blowing a trumpet and proclaiming the teachings of the church. Smith claims the angel told him about ancient religious texts buried near his home that became the foundations of his newly formed religion.

- **The Cross**

Perhaps the most recognizable religious symbol, the cross, represents the crucifixion of Christ. It has appeared throughout the ages and is a popular ornamental and significant symbol for many beliefs.

Secret Society Symbols

As the name suggests, these organizations worked in secret to achieve their goals. Since the ancient Greeks, they have been popular and are still part of society today. Some of these societies are collegiate, and some are more dedicated to influencing politicians and presidents. Whatever their aims, it has always been important that they have symbolic representations that make them identifiable to their members.

- **The Skull and Bones**

Founded in 1832, this secret society meets in a place called the Tomb, and the members are known as Bones men. The symbol is a classic skull and bones with the number 322 underneath it. The skull represents death, and the number 322 symbolizes the death of Demosthenes, which led to the emergence of plutocracy in Athens. The society members are picked from the elite and privileged of Yale and have been known to plunder other societies' treasures and keep them at the Tomb.

- **The Green Ribbon**

A simple green ribbon forming a loop is the symbol of a society called the Ribbon Society. Formed in Ireland, it was a Catholic group developed to fight the notorious Orangemen, the Protestant group dedicated to abolishing Catholicism in 19th century rural Ireland. They represented the agricultural workers who would often be subject to the tyranny of their Protestant landlords and kicked off their lands. The battles between the two factions were notoriously violent, and the society was active for twenty years.

- **Rosy Cross Symbol**

In the early 17th century in Europe, a secret society was formed to encourage the proletariat to learn about philosophy, astrology, and alchemy. The cavalry cross with a rose in the center represented the human form, with the rose representing consciousness. The Rosicrucians wrote texts and manifestos to encourage others to expand their knowledge, and their methods led to more educational secret societies, some of which are still in existence today.

- **The Square and Compass Symbol**

Local stonemasons banded together in the 14th century to form an organization to offer levels of stonemanship. The levels were graded from apprentice through to master mason, and they adopted the title Freemasons Society. As society evolved, they became synonymous with the promotion of goodwill and charity. Their teachings encouraged respectable behavior and the importance of boundaries. Secrecy is still a major feature of their ethos, and their symbol is the only way to identify members.

- **The Owl Symbol**

The Illuminati is one of the best-known secret societies that may or may not exist. The image of an owl on top of a book surrounded by a circle of laurel leaves represented the power of knowledge over religion and society-promoted enlightenment. The myths and folklore surrounding their influence are legendary; they are believed to have influenced the French Revolution and were mentioned by George Washington.

- **The Red Cross**

One of the most successful secret societies in history, the red cross is the symbol of the Knights Templar. These knights were the epitome of Christian beliefs and abstained from alcohol, bad language, and gambling while helping Christians on their quest to reach the Holy Land.

Viking Symbols

Although we have already discovered some of the more recognizable symbols from Viking lore, there are still some to uncover. Vikings were pagans who believed in an array of Gods and Goddesses, and they believed in using symbols to signify their allegiances. They also understood the importance of intimidation when facing their enemies. Their impressive appearance included a series of symbols that showed their strength and dedication.

- **Berserker Symbol**

This crude representation of the human form represented the berserker's unique way of fighting. They would appear in a trance and often be foaming at the mouth and gnashing their teeth when they faced their foes. They howled and literally ripped their enemies apart with their bare hands. Some reports stated that berserkers were the human form of bears when they fought, and this is why the Danish guard still wears bearskin hats as a tribute to their ancestors.

- **Wolf Symbol**

Wolves represent another group of warriors in Viking history named the Ulfhednar, who were the fighters chosen by the God Odin to represent him on the battlefield. They wore bearskins when battling and were just as fierce as the berserkers. After their death, they became the guardians of Valhalla.

- **The Boar Symbol**

Freya, the Norse Goddess of love, often rode a boar into battle, and the symbol represents her fierceness when faced with adversaries. It also represents the feast that awaited Viking warriors when they arrived home, symbolizing plenty, happiness, and peace.

Chapter 10: Creating Your Sigils

Working with magic is an intensely personal experience. You're working with universal energies to improve your life and make your environment better. Powerful magic should never be used to influence other people's lives or fate because the force you're creating is intense and should be filled with intentions seated in your psyche.

What Are the Benefits of Making Your Sigils?

Traditional sigils and signs have meaning and can be used to promote your intentions, but sometimes they can contain mixed messages. Because diverse cultures and beliefs attach varying meanings to symbols, it is always better to create your images and power them with your will.

The Benefits of Creating Your Sigils

- You feel more empowered; taking matters into your hands makes you feel energized and in charge of your destiny.
- You understand accountability. Gone are the days when you blame other people and circumstances for your fate.
- It gives you the opportunity to unleash your creative side. You may not be the best at art or calligraphy, but that doesn't matter. Art is fun, and getting creative is the perfect way to make a statement with your ideas.
- It motivates you. Creating a sigil is the first step to acknowledging your need to change and improve. Just like other journeys, the first step is the most important.
- There is hope in your life. Even the darkest times should contain light. Sigils create a firm intention to emerge from the darkness and find hope in times of desperation.

How to Create a Word Sigil

Begin with a statement of desire. Use powerful words and avoid negativity. Start a "wish list" to inspire your intentions if you're struggling with the process.

Start each sentence with the phrase "I wish" and then complete the phrase.

Examples of Wish List Staples

- I wish I could find a successful relationship

- I wish I were better at exercising
- I wish my diet were better
- I wish I had a better job

And so, the list goes on. Some modern practitioners believe that writing in the present tense makes the intention stronger. For example, "I feel at the peak of my personal fitness" when you wish for better fitness levels just as if it has already happened. The choice is yours, and both forms of language will work.

Now write the phrase down in full, removing any duplicates.

"I wish I had a better job" becomes "I, w, s, h, a, d, b, e, t, r, j, o," which is still too long, so remove the vowels. This leaves you with "w, s, h, d, b, t, r, j," which can be intertwined to create your sigil.

Pictorial Sigils

After all the information about symbolism, we already know the importance of imagery and pictures. Sigils are no different; they can contain images that signal your intention alongside words or replace them.

Here are some simple images to connect to the subconscious and trigger your intent:

- An artist's easel for creativity
- A pen and paper for help with writing or grammar
- Flame for help with passion or sex
- A heart for help with love, relationships, and family feuds
- Raindrops or snowflakes for connection to the element of water
- Pictures of a dollar bill for prosperity and wealth
- A shield or sword for protection
- Flowers, to represent the element earth
- An all-seeing eye to help your perception and insight
- A five-pointed star to represent the four elements combined with your inner self
- A crescent moon for help with feminine energy
- A dog for faithfulness

You can find suitable images almost everywhere. Let your creative juices flow, and check out glossy magazines for images to bring passion and fire to your sigil. If you feel more comfortable drawing your images, do that. Use colors and textures to add depth and extra layers to your intent.

Sate your intention above a circle containing your pictorial sigil for double energy. Use decorative alphabets or create your designs. These sigils will speak from your heart and show the universe you're ready to receive their energy.

Use Magic Grids to Create Your Sigil

The Archangel sigils are based on the letters on the Rose Wheel, and you can use that and other forms of magical grids to create your sigil. One of the most well-known examples is the Sator square, created by the Romans to generate designs for decorative amulets and talismans.

It is a super palindrome and works with five words in twenty-five squares that read the same in various directions.

SATOR

AREPO

TENET

OPERA

ROTAS

State your intent and then follow the path it creates within the Sator square. You may have noticed that all letters aren't represented, so just follow the ones that are contained in your intention.

Another popular way to turn your intent into a sigil is by using the Lo Shu Grid, also known as the magic square of Saturn. This grid is especially powerful because it represents the positive energy of the planet Saturn and is especially important for financial and business matters. Its planetary karma will influence your work and bring focus and direction to your life.

All the letters of the alphabet are written beneath the top line, which contains the numbers 1 – 9. A, J and S become 1, B, K and T are 2, and so on. Take a key phrase or word from your intention and use the grid to form a numerical representation.

For instance, "find love" becomes 6, 9, 5, 4, 3, 6, 4, 5. Now remove any repeated numbers, and you'll have 6, 9, 5, 4, and 3. Use a grid that contains all nine numbers and trace the path your numbers take you on. Start with the six and finish with the three.

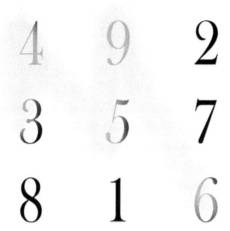

4   9   2

3   5   7

8   1   6

Automatic Writing Sigil

Sometimes we create the most powerful sigils using our energy and intent combined with a simple piece of paper and a pen. Seat yourself in a comfortable position and let the paper rest on your lap. Close your eyes and picture your intent. How will it improve your life? What will happen when you manifest your intentions. Hold the pen in your hand and let it move across the paper. When you have finished, you will have a rather chaotic and scribbled shape, but using your intuition, you will be able to identify images and shapes that can be recreated to form a sigil.

How to Charge Your Sigils

There are many ways to charge your sigil, but first, you need to disassociate with it. At the moment of creation, it is filled with emotional and spiritual energy that has come directly from you. It's time to let it rest and become a blank canvas for charging. Put it somewhere out of sight and mind, and go about your daily life until you feel it's time to charge it up and make it work for you. There is no fixed period for leaving your sigil in storage; it can be days, weeks, or even the full cycle of the moon. You will know when the time is right.

Now you have your blank canvas; it's time to charge your sigil with energy. Sexual, emotional, or spiritual energies work best. Positive vibes should power your sigil with the ability to influence your subconscious mind to achieve intentions.

Here Are Some Ideas on How to Charge Your Sigil

- Place it by the bed when you're being intimate with your partner or by yourself. Focus on the image at the point of orgasm to charge it with the power of your climax.
- Use meditation to focus your energy. While meditating, use the sigil as your focal point and invest your energy into its form.
- Use music to charge your sigil. Play music or use singing bowls to bring relaxing and emotional energy.
- Use crystals to charge your sigil just like you would with magical tools.
- Bring the energy of movement by dancing or clapping over the sigil. Make your movements energetic and filled with joy to achieve the best results.
- Use Moon or Sun water to bring heavenly energy. Charge a bowl of water by placing it in full daylight or moonlight. Sprinkle the sigil with drops of the anointed water to attract solar and lunar energy.

What to Do after Charging Your Sigil

There are two schools of thought about what to do after creating your charged sigil. Some people believe you should keep them in a safe place and use it when your subconscious needs a physical reminder of your intentions. Some creative ways to make permanent and semi-permanent sigils that will stay around as long as you dictate are:

- Take one of your shoes and use a pen to copy your sigil onto the sole or the inside of your shoe.
- Carve it into candles
- Draw onto your skin with mascara or a semi-permanent marker
- Carve into an ice cube so it melts
- Bury them outdoors
- Write on a bay leaf and use in cooking
- Carve on the bottom of a pie or in the icing on a cake
- Burn the image into wooden utensils
- Paint it on rocks
- Keep it in your purse or wallet

- Use it as a bookmark

If you adhere to the more formal beliefs of sigil magic, you will choose to destroy the sigil and release the intention so it can be fulfilled. This allows you to move on and let the magic work as soon as your sigil is cast into the universe. Make the destruction a special time; creating a ritual will help solidify the intention and increase the chance of success.

Here Are Some Powerful Ways to Cast Your Sigil

- Burn it. Use the paper you created it on – or transfer the image to a leaf or a candle – to burn it away
- Tear the paper up and let the wind scatter the pieces
- Send the sigil down a stream
- Bury it in a pot and put your favorite herb in the soil
- Erase it by using an eraser for pencil marks or Tippex (white correction fluid) for ink

Remember to record the sigils in your grimoire or Book of Spells to have a permanent reminder of your intentions despite the fact you have released them into the ether.

Now forget all about your sigil and go about your daily work. The intention will simmer in your subconscious and drive your actions to complete your goals.

List of Symbols

Alpha and Omega: The Greek alphabet's first and last letters.

Ankh: Egyptian hieroglyphical sign representing the key to life.

Apex: The height of a point, the symbol represents the highest point.

Bindi: Traditionally, red, yellow, or white. Bindi is a Sanskrit word for dot or point and symbolizes the beginning of creation.

Borromean Rings: Three interlocking circles that are a symbol of strength and unity.

Caduceus: The traditional symbol of Hermes, the messenger of God, is associated with medical organizations.

Chai: The symbol made by combining the Hebrew words *Chet* and *Yud* signifies "life."

Chalice: The holy cup of God, it also represents any sacred vessel.

Chi Rho: A combination of letters that represents Christendom and is the monogram of Christ.

Dove: The bird of peace.

Endless Knot: An infinite pattern that symbolizes the everlasting cycle of life.

Eye of God: Another version of the ever-seeing eye.

Eye of Horus: Egyptian eye symbol is often decorated with elaborate eyebrows.

Fleur-de-lis: Decorative symbol representing French ideals and literally means "flower of Lily."

Flower of Life: Symbol from sacred geometry consisting of multiple evenly-spaced circles that form a natural pattern similar to a flower.

Gordian Knot: Complex knots that signify intricate problems and extreme difficulty.

Hammer and Sickle: Traditionally a Russian symbol, the image represents the solidarity of union.

Hamsa: The image of a hand originating from the Hebrew word for hand.

Hand of Fatima: A decorated hand symbol related to the Goddess Fatima; it is a symbol of protection.

Hands of Svarog: Pro-Slavic symbol consisting of four hands forming a traditional cross.

Happy Human: The symbol of humanist organizations.

Heart: The ultimate symbol of love, joy, happiness, and passion.

Horned God: Wiccan representation of the two primary deities.

Hunab Ku: Ancient Mayan, a symbol of the Supreme God or Being. It symbolizes the encompassing belief in God.

Ichthus: The fish, Ichthus, is how early Christians identify other faith members.

Inanna's Knot: An elaborate symbol that represents abundance and prosperity.

Infinity: A mathematical and spiritual symbol of the never-ending.

Kali Yantra: The symbol of transformation and rebirth. It represents the Goddess Kali and is used in meditation.

Lotus: The sacred flower of Hinduism, Buddhism, and Jainism. The lotus is the flower of peace and love.

Maltese Cross: The iconic cross of St. John is often associated with courage and bravery.

Menorah: The Jewish candelabra that symbolizes the seven days of creation with the Sabbath represented by the central lamp.

Merkaba: The Hebrew symbol for chariot that means "light body and spirit."

Om: The Sanskrit symbol of the vibration that powers the whole universe, commonly used in meditation practices.

Ouroboros: A snake or dragon swallowing their tail symbolizes eternity and everlasting life.

Papal Cross: The Catholic symbol of Christ.

Pentacle: A five-pointed figure that symbolizes four elements topped with the element of spirit.

Pentagram: The star-shaped symbol of faith in Wiccan beliefs was also used in ancient Greece and Babylon for protection.

Red Cross: Associated with medical emergencies and organizations.

Sacred Chaos: A symbol of Discordianism, which teaches that order and chaos are all man-made.

Scarab: An ancient Egyptian symbol represented by the scarab beetle.

Skull and Bones: The symbol of a notorious secret society founded at Yale

University.

Sri Yantra: A mystical diagram that represents nine interlocking triangles with the power to change your life forever by using the energies of Shiva and Raj, important Indian deities.

Star of David: The Jewish symbol of identity comprised of two equilateral triangles forming a six-sided star.

Sun Wheel: Also referred to as a solar cross, this symbol was associated with the God Odin and was a Nordic symbol of the sun.

The Labyrinth: The maze is an everlasting symbol of the cycle of life and our recurring existence on Earth.

Thors Hammer: The mighty tool of Thor, the hammer is a protective symbol of strength and control.

Thunderbird: The native American symbol of power, war, and victory, this bird-like image is widely used and placed at the top of totem poles.

Tree of Life: The archetypal symbol of the world's religions and philosophies. The connection between the heavens and Earth connects all of creation.

Triple Moon: Representing the three phases of the moon, waxing, full, and waning. It is the symbol of the Goddess and her feminine energy.

Triquetra: The Celtic knot is a symbol of unity, rebirth, and the connection between life and death.

Triskele: Three interlocked spirals. The triskele is the Irish symbol for synergy that focuses on the connection between natural order and balance.

Vesica Pisces: Two overlapping circles form an almond-shaped center. Its origins lie in Africa and the East and symbolize the womb and the power of birth.

Yin Yang: The Chinese black and white symbol of combined male and female energy.

Conclusion

Symbols are integral to most human communities; they are a central aspect of the meaning of many processes embedded in our everyday lives. Signs and symbols play an essential role in forming implications related to cultural beliefs, religious principles, spiritual moments, and institutional or ideological powers that we use, stand by, or adopt in our lives. This role may be played directly or indirectly. Symbols are even necessary for the survival of the current global economic system we live within, fueling prominent advertisement and governmental campaigns that work to make different impressions in larger popular society. Learning how to see through, understand, and eventually harness the power of the symbols we find around us is crucial if we want to further develop our spiritual connection and alignment to the universe and the events that unfold within – and in relation to – it.

Now you have the necessary introductory knowledge to start your journey. You have the tools for deeply understanding symbols and other images, drastically improving your communication skills, and becoming part of the universal union. There are no downsides to this skill; you will become more receptive to the world's subliminal messages and have a better and more open perspective on life and the importance of communication. Go forward; be receptive and ready to take in the energy that coexists with us and guides our lives in certain moments; the universe is waiting for you. Good luck with your new journey!

Printed in Great Britain
by Amazon

36215890R00067